Ludwig Steiger

Timber Construction

BAS

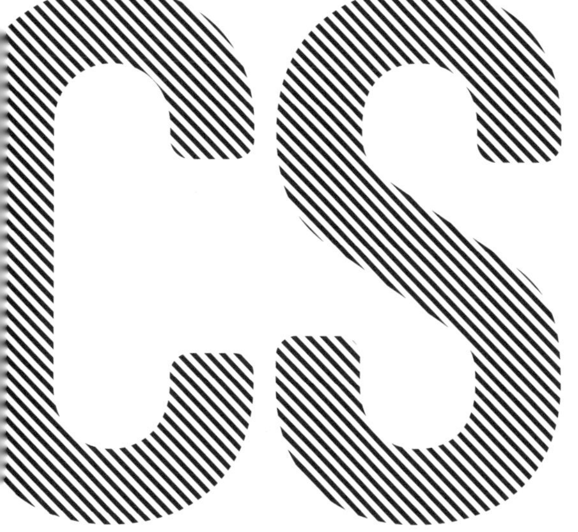

Ludwig Steiger

Timber Construction

Third edition

BIRKHÄUSER
BASEL

Contents

Foreword

Wood is one of humankind's oldest and most elemental building materials, and has lost none of its appeal or validity. In many cultures and climates timber dominates over brick as the choice for house building.

In recent times, timber construction has experienced a revival because wood components are basically CO_2-neutral and, compared to solid components such as those made of concrete, they consume significantly less energy over their life cycle. It follows that wood is a very sustainable building material and is a renewable resource. Wood is a living, light, simply worked material, and houses with a character all their own can be built from it. But timber construction has some particular characteristics that make it unlike other materials in construction. So architects need special knowledge about wood and the rules for timber construction, in order to develop quality designs that do justice to the material.

The first designs in an architecture course are often for timber houses, as this material is ideal for learning construction methods and principles in a way that is close to practice. The author therefore begins by explaining the qualities of timber as a natural building material and the construction products developed from it, then moves on to the commonest timber construction systems and their specific rules. The construction rules learned in this way are then applied to all the connections and transitions for the building components, and are elaborated using examples.

This third edition of the book now includes details on solid panel construction, as in recent years this building method has gained in popularity as a replacement for solid construction. A number of building codes now allow timber buildings up to the high-rise building limit; when the timber components are combined with reinforced concrete elements, it is possible to create multistory timber buildings that fully comply with fire safety regulations.

The timber construction volume enables students to gain a general insight into individual timber construction systems, to understand them in detail and to distinguish them from each other. Armed with this knowledge, you can select the most sensible system for your design and apply your knowledge constructively.

Bert Bielefeld, Editor

Introduction

In a 1937 essay on training architects, Mies van der Rohe said: "Where does the structure of a house or building show with such clarity as in the timber structures of the ancients, where do we see the unity of material, construction and form so clearly? Here the wisdom of whole generations lies concealed. What a sense of material and what expressive power speaks from these buildings! What warmth they exude, and how beautiful they are! They sound like old songs." This statement by one of the 20th century's most important architects conveys both the fascination of timber construction and the challenge it presents.

The living material, the different kinds of timber, the large number of timber construction systems, the sophisticated stratification of the building components and the way they are jointed require a great deal of knowledge if this building material is to be used appropriately in student design work.

Unlike the monolithic massive construction procedures with which students are familiar, timber construction works by assembling members, following a fixed order, and working with a defined structural grid. In terms of planning, this means a more systematic approach is needed, and also a greater degree of detailing and drawing work. This book introduces students to timber construction in three stages. First, readers are familiarized with the material wood and its properties, then the most important construction systems and their characteristic joints, finally assembling components and fitting them together. Our presentation is based around simple, manageable building solutions that are suitable for identifying the key problems of any particular timber structure. Large-scale loadbearing systems, bridges or hall structures that are ideally suited to timber construction are not considered, but information on further reading is provided.

One particular difficulty in presenting timber construction should be mentioned, although it can also be seen as a great opportunity. Timber construction techniques can be said to be in a state of flux. To complement the existing traditional systems, the industry is introducing a large number of new materials and technologies to timber construction.

This book aims to structure this very broad field and provide an overview. This will involve first of all passing on established knowledge and tried-and-tested structures, but there will be at least an indication of new building materials and technical developments.

Building material

WOOD

Several hundred varieties of wood are used on a large scale all over the world. They all look different and have their own particular properties. Many of them are used for finishing, and in furniture manufacture. Relatively little coniferous timber is used in wooden buildings, so beginners do not have to be timber experts in order to build with timber. The important thing is to understand its anatomical structure, and to know about the fundamental physical properties of this material.

Growth

When using wood, it is important to be aware that a piece of timber, a beam or plank is part of a vegetable organism, a tree, and that its growth and quality are influenced by its surroundings. No one piece of wood is identical to another. Its properties depend in the first place on the kind of tree, and in the second on its position within the trunk.

Cells

The trunk consists of longitudinal tubiform cells, which are responsible for transporting nutrients as the tree grows. The cell walls enclosing the tubiform cavity are made up of cellulose and lignin (filler substance). The structure of the cell walls and the cell framework determine the strength of the wood. Unlike building materials such as non-reinforced concrete or masonry blocks, wood has a directional structure, corresponding to the path taken by nutrients from the trunk to the branches. ○

Cell growth takes place around the centre of the trunk, called the pith cavity, the oldest part of the trunk. It takes place in the form of annual growth phases, generally lasting from April to September in temperate zones, and creates annual rings.

○ **Note:** The loadbearing properties of a timber construction component are fundamentally determined by the loading across the direction of the fibre, the grain, or parallel to it. Plans must therefore contain information about the installation direction. In sections, the hatching makes it clear whether the timber is cut across or parallel to the grain.

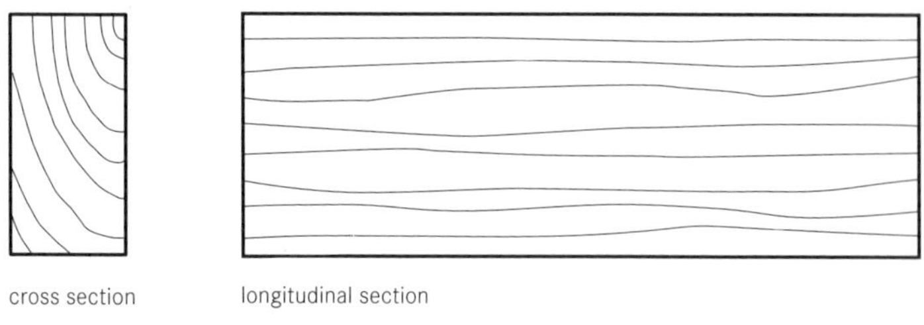

Fig. 1: Timber cut crossways and parallel

Early wood, late wood

Within these rings, the softer early wood is formed in the spring from large-pored cells, and the more solid late wood with thick-walled cells follows in the autumn. The proportion of late wood essentially determines the strength of the timber.

Sapwood, heart

This growth process can be read very simply by looking at the cross section of the trunk. According to the type of wood, the outer area, the sapwood, is more or less clearly distinct from the older, inner section, the heartwood. The heartwood has no supply role to fulfil, and is thus drier than the sap-bearing parts. Differences between heartwood and sapwood make it possible to divide timber types into

- heartwood trees
- close-textured trees
- sapwood trees

Heartwood trees have a dark core and light sapwood. They are considered to be particularly weather-resistant. They include oak, larch, pine and walnut.

Close-textured trees show no colour difference between sapwood and heartwood, simply differences in moisture content. Both are equally light-coloured; the heart is dry, the sapwood moist. This applies to spruce, fir, beech and maple, for example.

Sapwood trees, on the other hand, show no difference in either colour or moisture content. They include birch, alder and poplar.

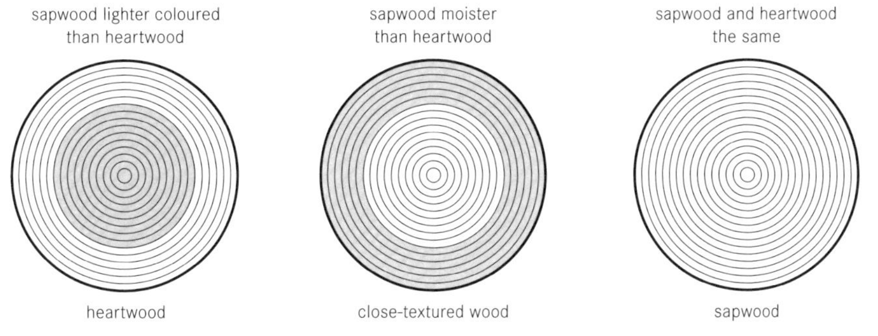

Fig. 2: Heartwood, close-textured and sapwood tree (trunk cross sections)

Timber moisture

Almost all physical properties of wood are influenced by moisture content. Its weight depends on this, its resistance to fire and pests, its loadbearing capacity and above all, its dimensional stability and consistency.

Shrinking, swelling

Wood swells and shrinks with changing moisture conditions. When wood dries, its volume is reduced, which is called shrinkage, and the reverse process, which causes an increase in volume, is known as swelling. This takes place because both the cell cavities and the cell walls contain water. As a hygroscopic material, wood is able to give off or absorb moisture according to the ambient conditions. This is also known as timber movement.

Moisture content must be specified for construction timber. Here a distinction is made between:

Green	more than 30% wood moisture
Semi-dry	more than 20% but maximum 30% wood moisture
Dry	up to 20% wood moisture

Construction timber should always be installed in a dry state, if possible at the moisture level expected at the location. Timber equilibrium moisture indicates the moisture levels at which only small changes of dimensions take place. For rooms this means:

Closed on all sides, heated	9 ± 3%
Closed on all sides, unheated	12 ± 3%
Covered, open	15 ± 3%
Structures exposed to weathering on all sides	18 ± 6%

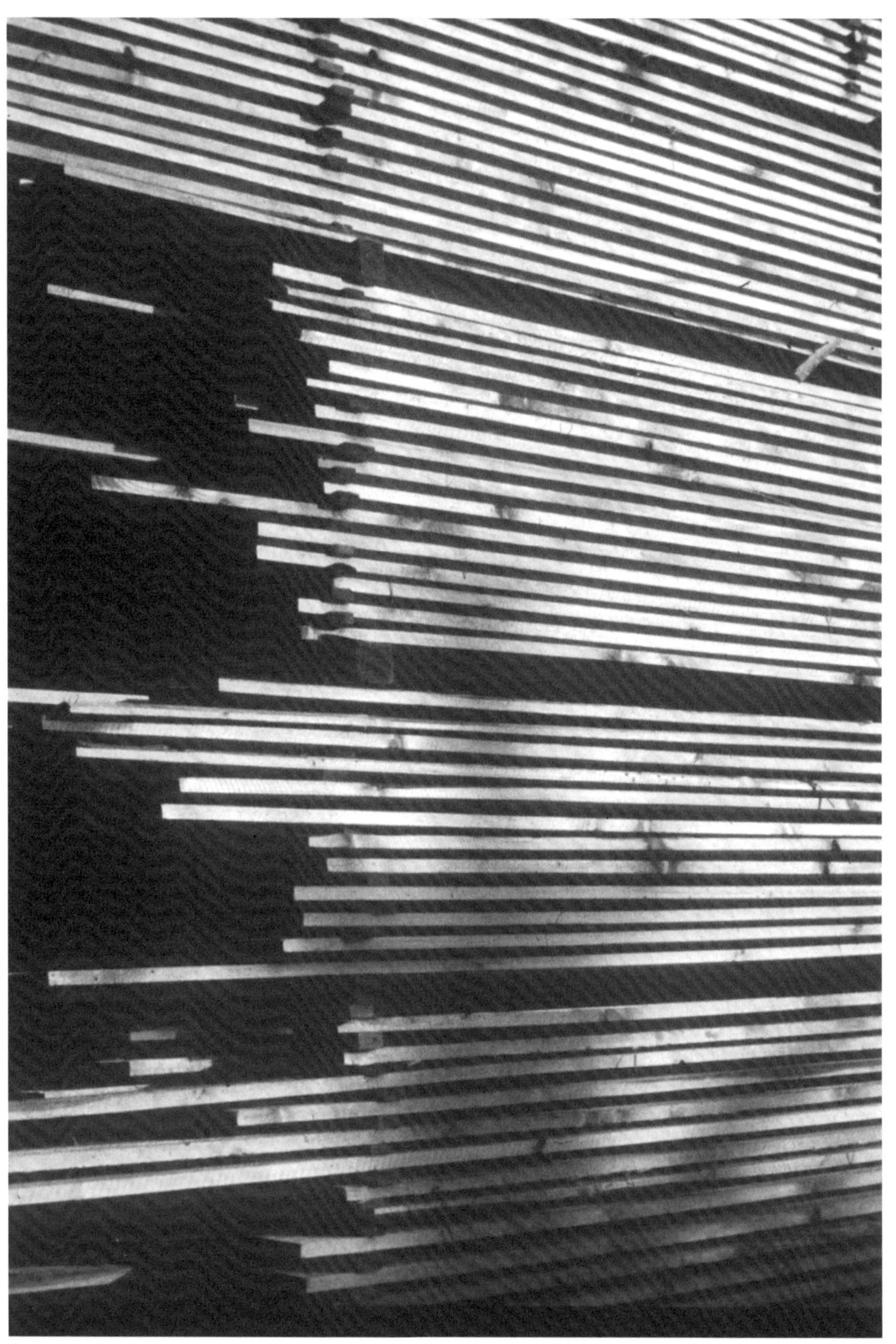

Wood moisture indicates the percentage of water contained, with reference to absolutely dry wood. But movement in wood is not a single, once-and-for-all process; it happens after the timber has been installed as well. According to the ambient atmospheric humidity, which is lower in winter than in summer, timber shrinks and swells seasonally as well. ○

Types of cut

Because of the difference between the water content of sapwood and heartwood, as well as between early and late wood inside the annual rings, shrinkage rates differ, and thus the cut timber becomes distorted. The key factor here is its position in the trunk.

Timber can be cut tangentially to the heart or radially, i.e. at right angles to the annual rings, and this affects the degree of volume change. According to the type of wood, the degree of shrinkage is usually more than double for tangentially cut than for radially cut wood. Longitudinal shrinkage is negligible.

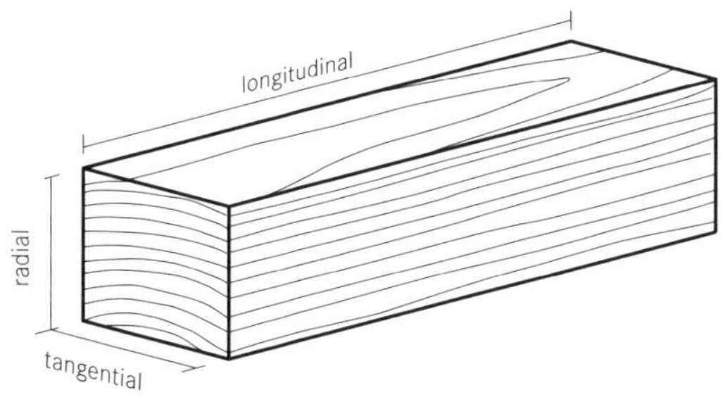

Fig. 3: Isometric drawing of squared timber showing radial and tangential sides

○ **Note:** One of the most important rules for timber construction is that wood must always be installed to allow for movement caused by shrinking and swelling, e.g. by leaving sufficiently large gaps between the timber components. Ideally a form board should be fastened with one screw only, in the middle or at the edge, so that the wood can move crosswise to the fibre direction (see Chapter Components, External wall).

The difference in volume change also means that planks or squared timber cut from one trunk at right angles distort differently. Tangential planks bend (bow) outwards on the side away from the heart, due to the shortening of the annual rings. Only the centre board, the heart board, remains straight, although it becomes thinner in the sapwood area. The grey frames in Figure 4 show the reduction in volume as cut timber shrinks.

Properties

Wood's finely porous structure makes it a relatively good material for insulation. The thermal conductivity coefficient of the coniferous timbers (softwoods) spruce, pine and fir is 0.13 W/mK, that of the deciduous timbers (hardwoods) beech and ash 0.23 W/mK. So in comparison with brick at 0.44 W/mK or concrete at 1.8 W/mK, wood has considerably better thermal insulation properties than many other building materials.

In contrast, wood's thermal expansion, unlike steel or concrete, is so slight that it can be disregarded for building purposes.

Gross density

Wood has a low gross density, so its thermal storage capacity is less than for solid building materials such as masonry or concrete. The thermal storage coefficient of spruce and fir is 350 Wh/m^3K, whereas that of standard concrete is 660 Wh/m^3K. This is particularly problematic for summer thermal protection. The thermal compensation between cool night and daytime warming is less in timber than for solid structures. The lower gross density also means that wood has a low sound insulation coefficient, but absorbs sound well because of its open cells.

Thermal storage capacity and sound insulation can be achieved only by incorporating heavy building materials as well, i.e. materials with a greater gross density, such as plasterboards or fibre cement, in the walls, or by correspondingly heavy floor coverings.

O **Note:** The side of a piece of tangentially cut timber furthest from the heart is designated the left-hand side, and the side facing the heart the right-hand side. The anticipated deformation should be taken into account when the timber is used for building.

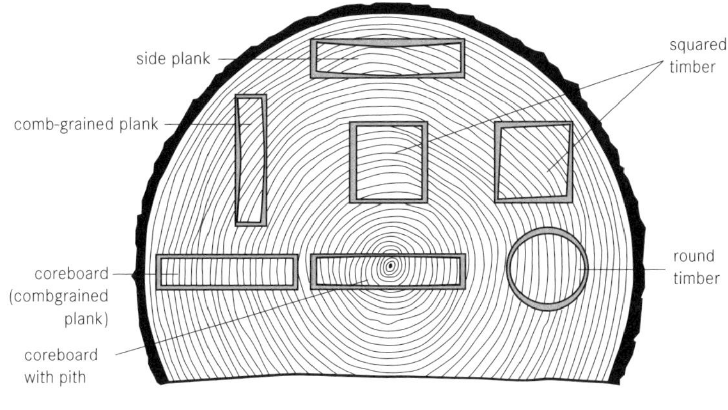

Fig. 4: Cross section of trunk, types of cut

Fire prevention

Although wood is a flammable material (normally flammable), its behaviour in fire is not as problematic as would seem at a first glance. Wood with a large cross section burns relatively slowly and evenly from outside to inside because of the accumulating charcoal layer, so that it takes time to lose its loadbearing capacity. This is quite different from a steel girder, for example, which is not combustible, but deforms at high temperatures and loses its loadbearing capacity.

The burning rate of wood becomes lower the moister the wood is. Across the grain the speed is around 0.6–0.8 mm/min for softwood, for oak about 0.4 mm/min. In addition, behaviour in fire depends on external form. The greater the surface area at the same volume, the lower the fire resistance. This is particularly marked in the case of shrinkage cracks in solid wood. For this reason laminated wood without cracks will resist fire for longer and times can be calculated more accurately than for solid wood.

O **Note:** Gross density indicates the strength of a building material. It depends on the weight of the material, and is given in kg/m^3. The gross density of softwood is 450–600 kg/m^3, of European hardwoods 700 kg/m^3, of overseas hardwoods up to 1000 kg/m^3. In comparison with this, standard concrete comes in at 2000–2800 kg/m^3.

So with appropriate dimensioning, wood can meet fire prevention requirements. ○

Loadbearing capacity

Unlike masonry, which is ideally suited for dealing with load and pressure, wood can absorb compressive and tensile forces to an equal extent. But because of the above-mentioned tubular cell structure, the direction in which the force is applied is crucial. Parallel to the grain, in other words along its longitudinal axis, wood can absorb approximately four times as much compressive force than across the grain. The response to tensile force is even more extreme. Figure 5 shows the appropriate strengths for coniferous wood (S 10) as admissible tensions in N/mm^2 according to German standards.

For construction this means that, as far as possible, the timber should be installed so that the load is placed on its efficient longitudinal axis, where it can absorb compressive and tensile forces.

In general, loadbearing capacity depends on the proportion of thick-walled timber cells, and thus on the density of the wood. Hard deciduous timber such as oak is thus particularly suitable for compressive loading, as a sill or threshold timber, for example, while long-fibred coniferous timber is more suitable for dealing with bending loads.

As a building material that grows and shows all the irregularities of nature, the expected loadbearing capacity of construction timber is not guaranteed from the outset. It is therefore sorted visually and mechanically according to certain characteristics such as the number and size of the branches, any deviations in the fibres, cracks, gross density and elasticity, and then graded for sale.

Sorting

In Germany, loadbearing construction timber is divided into three sorting classes or grades, and the strength to be used for static calculations is stated in terms of these grades. > Tab. 1

○ **Note:** In Germany the fire resistance classes F30 B, F60 B or F90 B indicate that a component will retain its ability to function in case of fire for 30, 60 or 90 minutes, respectively.

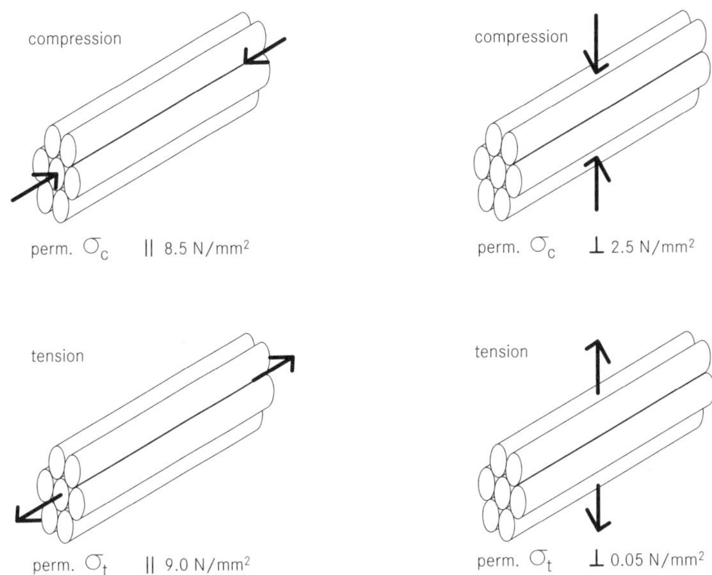

Fig. 5: Admissible compressive/tensile forces

Tab. 1: Sorting classes and grades in Germany

Sorting class	Grade	Loadbearing capacity
S 13	I	higher than average
S 10	II	normal
S 7	III	low

In other countries, standardization can be even more sophisticated. In America, all construction timber is marked with a stamp providing the following information: grade, quality control organization, sawmill number, timber type, moisture content, E module, bending strength and use.

This makes allocating wood on the building site and building supervision control considerably easier.

TIMBER CONSTRUCTION PRODUCTS

The timber construction products introduced below start with solid wood and its production and continue with timber products in which the structure of the starting material is significantly changed. They finish with building boards, which contain other bonding materials and substances such as cement and plaster.

Solid wood

The term solid wood includes round timber with the bark removed or cut softwood or hardwood. Construction timber is available from sawmills as stock squared timber in particular cross sections and lengths. Timber is classified as laths, planks, boards and squared timber according to the ratio of thickness to width. > Tab. 2

Dimensions

The thicknesses and widths specified in Table 3 are the current dimensions for laths, planks, and boards. Other measurement systems differ only slightly from these dimensions in millimetres.

Construction timber is normally used as sawn, in other words unplaned. In the case of planks and boards planed on both sides, e.g. for visible interior use, approx. 2.5 mm should be deducted from the given dimensions in each case. The lengths extend from 1.5 to 6 m in 25 and 30 cm steps.

Stock squared timber is available in whole-centimetre dimensions with square and rectangular cross sections. The cross sections listed in Table 4 are the preferred dimensions.

American stock squared timber is based on the inch (25.4 mm) as a unit. Starting with a minimum width of 2 inches, slender cross sections emerge, principally adapted to American timber frame construction's close rib positioning. > Chapter Construction, Timber frame construction and Tab. 5

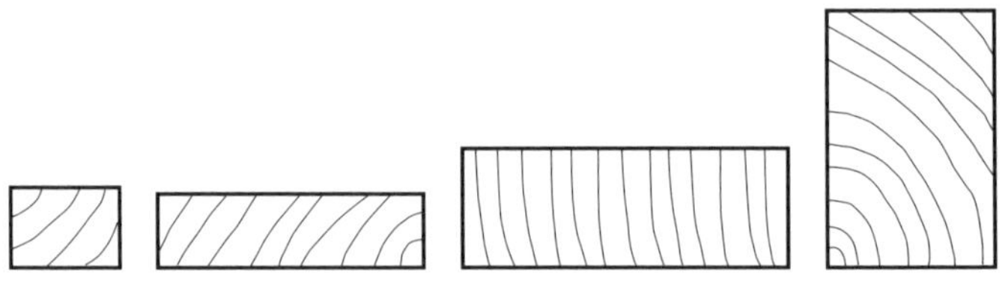

Fig. 6: Cross sections: lath, plank, board, squared timber

Tab. 2: Cross sections for lath, plank, board, squared timber

	Thickness t	**Width w**
	Height h [mm]	[mm]
Lath	t ≤ 40	w < 80
Plank	t ≤ 40	w ≥ 80
Board	t > 40	w > 3d
Squared timber	w ≤ h ≤ 3w	w > 40

Tab. 3: Customary timber cross sections

Lath cross sections	24/48, 30/50, 40/60
Thicknesses for planks	16, 18, 22, 24, 28, 38
Thicknesses for boards	44, 48, 50, 63, 70, 75
Thicknesses for planks/boards	80, 100, 115, 120, 125,140, 150, 160, 175

Tab. 4: Customary dimensions of squared timber

6/6, 6/8, 6/12, 6/14, 6/16, 6/18
8/8, 8/10, 8/12, 8/16, 8/18
10/10, 10/12, 10/20, 10/22, 10/24
12/12, 12/14, 12/16, 12/20, 12/22
14/14, 14/16, 14/20
16/16, 16/18, 16/20
18/22, 18/24
20/20, 20/24, 20/26

Tab. 5: American timber sizes in inches

Widths	2, 2½, 3, 3½, 4, 4½
Heights	2, 3, 4, 5, 6, 8, 10, 12, 14, 16

The commonest timber types in Central and Northern Europe include spruce, fir, pine, larch and Douglas fir. In America they include Douglas fir, red cedar, Caroline pine and pitch pine.

Solid timber products

The following solid timber products are produced by further refining and finishing solid timber.

Solid construction timber (SCT) is sorted to the usual standards for strength, then also sorted and specially classified for appearance. It thus

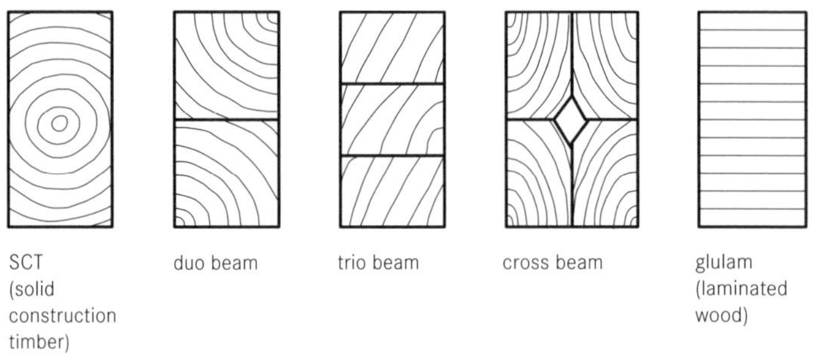

Fig. 7: SCT, duo and trio beams, cross beams, laminated boards

meets specific requirements in terms of loadbearing capacity, appearance, dimensional and formal stability, moisture content, limitations on crack width, and surface quality. Wedge finger jointing, i.e. gluing the wedge-shaped tenons on the ends, makes it possible to supply any required length. It is available in the customary cross section dimensions for stock squared timber.

Similarly improved solid timber quality is achieved with duo or trio beams, for which two or three boards or squared timbers are glued together on the flat side with parallel grain.

Cross beams are made up of quarter timbers glued together with parallel grain. Here the outside of the round timber segments is turned inwards, thus creating a central tube inside the rectangular cross section that runs through the full length of the beam.

Glue-laminated timber (glulam) meets very rigorous requirements in terms of formal stability and loadbearing capacity. It consists of softwood boards glued together under pressure, on the broad side, with parallel grain. Artificial resin adhesives based on phenol, resorcin, melamine or polyurethane are used to achieve waterproof adhesion. These show up in different colours externally in the glued joints, ranging from dark brown to light.

The boards are dried before gluing and planed, and any flaws in the wood are removed mechanically. The laminated gluing means that there is next to no deformation of the timber cross section. Glue-laminated timber is often used for wide loadbearing structure spans because it can be supplied in cross sections of up to 200 cm, and up to 50 m long.

Timber-based products

Timber-based products are a particularly economical use of wood, as they even redeploy timber processing waste such as shavings and fibres, as well as timber components such as boards, members, veneers and veneer strips.

Manufacture is industrial, by pressing with artificial resin adhesives or mineral bonding agents. This means that the original product is considerably enhanced. The irregular qualities of the wood are homogenized. The static properties and the tensions to which they can be submitted can be established much more precisely for timber products than for solid wood. Timber products also shrink and swell considerably less than solid wood.

Timber products are usually supplied in panel form in standard dimensions, e.g. panels 125 cm wide. ■

Gluing

Timber-based products are classified all over the world according to the way in which they are glued, to provide information about how the particular product responds to moisture. In Germany, the classification shown in Table 6 applies.

American timber construction has four gluing classes. > Tab. 7

Tab. 6: Timber product classifications for Germany

V20	unsuitable for moisture
V100	suitable for short-term exposure to moisture
V100 G	suitable for long-term exposure to moisture; protected against fungi

Tab. 7: Product classes in American timber production

Exterior	persistent exposure to moisture
Exposure 1	high resistance in periodic rain, not suitable for long-term exposure
Exposure 2	normal exposure to moisture
Interior	for protected interiors not exposed to moisture

■ **Tip:** To guarantee economical exploitation of the panels, the construction grid must be fixed at the panel stage to allow as little waste as possible. Given a panel width of 125 cm, the same distance between axes, or half that at 62.5 cm or even one third at 41.6 cm will offer the most economical approach.

Both Exterior and Exposure 1 correspond to the German V100 classification, while Interior is comparable with V20.

Timber products can be classified by component nature as

- plywood and laminated boards
- chip products
- fibre products

Plywood and laminated boards

Plywood and laminated boards consist of at least three layers of wood glued on top of each other, with the grain direction set crossways.

This transverse arrangement of the layers, also known as crossbanding, prevents the wood from moving and gives the panel the necessary strength and stability in every direction. Plywood and laminated boards are thus particularly suitable for reinforcing timber structures and loadbearing walls. They can also be used for exterior work, provided the correct adhesive is used, although edges are particularly susceptible to damp, and should be covered or sealed if installed as facade panels.

For veneer plywood, the veneers are glued on top of each other in three, five, seven or nine layers, according to the thickness of the board (8–33 mm). Veneer plywood, with at least five layers and more than 12 mm thick, is also called multiplex board.

Strip board and blockboard, also known as coreboard, is plywood that consists of at least three layers with a middle layer of strips lying crossways to the covering veneers and giving the board particularly good loadbearing properties.

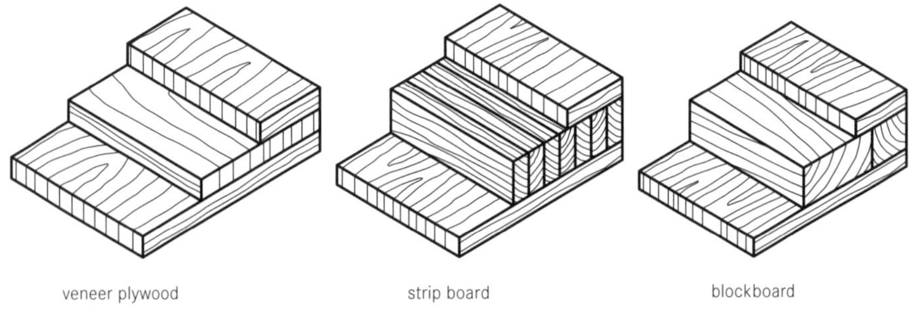

Fig. 8: Isometric diagram of veneer plywood, strip board, blockboard

The most commonly used plywood and laminated boards include:

- Veneer plywood
- Strip and blockboard
- Three- and five-ply boards
- Laminated boards
- Multiplex boards

Chip products

Chipboards use the waste products of the timber industry. Boards are made by compressing sawdust and plane shavings with adhesives. Unlike plywood, this does not produce continuous layers, but an intricate undirected structure. They can be used either as reinforcing planking > Chapter Construction, Reinforcement for walls, floors, ceilings and roofs, or fitted in above-floor constructions as dry screed.

OSB

A type of chipboard that is often used in the building industry is oriented strand board, so called because of its directed structure of relatively long (approx. 35 × 75 mm) rectangular chips or shavings. Because its direction changes layer by layer, it has directed mechanical properties like plywood. This means that very high strengths can be achieved, twice to three times as high as normal chipboard.

The following chip products are commonly used:

- Flat pressboard
- Laminated strand board (LSL)
- Oriented strand board (OSB)
- Extruded pressboard

Fibreboard

The components of fibreboard are even smaller than for timber chip products. The original coniferous timber is so reduced in size that the wood structure is no longer recognizable. The product is manufactured wet without bonding agents using various procedures with and without pressure, and with and without adhesive, as follows:

- Woodfibre insulation board
- Softboard (SB)
- Bituminized wood fibreboard
- Medium hardwood fibreboard

Or using a dry process, with adhesive added:

- Medium density fibreboard (MDF)
- High density fibreboard (HDF)
- Hardwood fibreboard

Board made by the wet process is usually softboard for use in interiors, for sound and heat insulation and as roof formwork. Medium density fibreboard (MDF) is very popular for furniture construction and internal finishing because of its homogeneous structure. High density and hard fibreboards are used mainly for facade cladding.

Structural board

Board products that, unlike organically bound timber products, are bound inorganically are known as structural board. The starting material contains only as a certain proportion of wood, or none at all. They are divided into boards bound by cement:

- Cement-bound chipboard
- Fibre cement board

And boards bound with plaster:

- Plaster-bound chipboard
- Plasterboard
- Fibreboard

Cement-bound boards are characterized primarily by their high level of resistance to water and frost, and to attack by fungi and insects. They are therefore used largely as facade material, right down to the base area in contact with the ground. They are also suitable as reinforcing, effective boarding in timber construction.

On the other hand, plaster-bound boards are for interior use only, plasterboard mainly as cladding for walls and ceilings, and fibreboard commonly in several layers as screed in floor construction. Plaster- and fibreboard can be used for boarding external walls if they are permanently protected against the weather.

TIMBER PROTECTION

Unlike the mineral materials masonry and concrete, wood, as an organic material is subject to damage from vegetable (fungi) and animal (insect) pests. If it is attacked, the outward form of the timber can be affected, but also its loadbearing capacity, to the extent of completely destroying the building. Timber protection is thus of the utmost importance in timber construction. Pests

Fungi need cellulose in order to develop. They flourish particularly in wet, warm, unventilated areas. Timber moisture content of at least 20% is needed for the ensuing wood rot.

Insects, mainly beetles, use timber in the sapwood area of conifers in particular to feed and house their larvae. Termites are among the insects that are most destructive of wood. They live mainly in the tropics and subtropics, as well as in America and the southern European Mediterranean countries. Infestation with termites is not visible from the outside: termites construct a system of passageways inside the wood in order to avoid loss of water. Buildings or furniture that have been infested collapse suddenly when a load is place on them.

Timber protection is known as control in the case of wood that has already been infested, or as preventive protection, to make sure that no infestation takes place.

When planning timber building, preventive timber protection is the most important. Essentially there are three measures available:

- Choice of wood
- Structural timber protection
- Chemical timber protection

Choice of wood

Only timber that has been well dried and appropriately stored should be considered. Care should be taken that the moisture content is less than 20%.

Many countries' classifications also specify which types of wood are naturally resistant to insect damage. These include the heartwood > Chapter Building material, Growth of teak, greenheart, bongossi, oak and false acacia. In America, recommended types include the heartwood of black locust, black walnut and redwood. These woods can be used without chemical protection in parts of the building where particular exposure to moisture is expected. But chemical timber protection is essential if there is to be contact with soil.

Structural timber protection

Planners are the key figures in structural timber protection. The design, and particularly the details of it, should be laid out to avoid permanent moisture penetration of wood and wooden building sections. The topic will be discussed again in the detailed treatment of bases, windows and roof edges in the chapter Components. ■

Chemical timber protection

Chemical timber protection should be used only when all other timber protection methods have been exhausted.

Possible chemical timber preservatives include water-soluble, solvent-based or oily coatings or impregnation materials. To avoid environmental pollution, timber preservatives should be applied only in closed facilities, for example by boiler pressure processes or trough impregnation. Only cut surfaces and drilled holes may be treated on the building site.

Chemical timber preservatives are used according to the static function of the building components. Here we distinguish between

- loadbearing and reinforcing timber sections
- non-loadbearing timbers that are not dimensionally stable
- non-loadbearing timbers that are dimensionally stable timbers for windows and doors

For loadbearing members, preventive treatment is necessary. Local laws determine whether this can be in chemical form, e.g. according to the degree of risk and corresponding allocation to a risk class. ○

No chemical preservation measures need be taken under certain conditions and when using resistant timber types.

■ **Tip:** Not only in timber construction, but particularly there, the following points should be noted:

1. Keep damp out (roof projections, recesses, dripboards).
2. Ensure that water can run off (sloping horizontal surfaces).
3. Let air in to wood that has become damp (ventilation spaces).

○ **Note:** Timber components touching the soil are subject to the highest risk. Contact with the soil and thus permanent exposure of the timber to moisture should be avoided in any structure. A base zone of about 30 cm separating the wood from the ground is typical of timber structures.

Doors and windows

Windows and external doors are non-loadbearing but dimensionally stable components that permit very low tolerances if they are to function properly. They need particular protection against damp. But it is possible to manage without chemical treatment when heartwood with a certain permanent strength is used.

Non-loadbearing components that are not dimensionally stable do not have to work within close tolerances. These include overlapping timber cladding, fences and pergolas. They can be constructed without preservatives and without being painted, provided it is accepted that they will become increasingly grey. Chemical timber preservatives should under no circumstances be used on large areas of interior timber.

Construction

"Wooden buildings have to be constructed, stone buildings can be drawn," the Swiss architect Paul Artaria once wrote. This somewhat provocative statement was not intended to deny masonry construction its structural legitimacy, but rather to indicate the special requirements of building with wood, the logic of rod-based structures and the systematics of timber jointing.

STRUCTURAL STABILITY

Timber construction offers several answers or construction systems to meet the elementary requirement of structural stability, with specific loadbearing mechanisms and their associated nodal complexes at interfaces.

A brief introduction to the static requirements of timber construction systems is followed by an introduction to the most important timber construction systems in this second part of the book.

Loadbearing system

The structural stability of a building depends on various factors. First, the material used must have an adequate loadbearing capacity and appropriate dimensions to absorb the vertical loads from walls, roof and ceiling. The subsoil must also be able to take such loads.

Horizontal forces also affect all buildings, mainly from wind loads, but also impact loads that affect the structure horizontally. ○

Reinforcement

One way of handling horizontal forces is restraint or rigid fixing. > Fig. 10 The supporting members are fixed into the foundations so that they are flexurally rigid, to prevent them from shifting sideways or becoming deformed. The simplest and most primitive form of restraint is ramming the sharpened tip of a timber support into the ground. In reinforced concrete construction, restraining the concrete columns in

○ **Note:** This subject is examined in detail in *Basics Loadbearing Systems* by Alfred Meistermann, Birkhäuser, Basel 2007.

bucket foundations has become accepted practice. Wood protection requirements make this kind of fixing problematical in timber construction.

The appropriate way to reinforce a timber construction is by making walls and ceilings into a rigid structure in all three dimensions. Imagine a cardboard box whose side walls can be pushed relatively easily into a rhomboid shape until the lid is added. It is only when this third section, the horizontal lid, is put in place that a stable, reinforced structure is created. > Fig. 9 O

Diagonal bracing

The basic element of a reinforced surface is the fixed triangle. In timber construction, it is relatively easy to fasten members together in the form of a triangle. This is known as triangular bracing, and makes the rectangular wall frame into a fixed plate.

Figure 10 shows the various ways of making a plate structure: a) using two compression members, whose competence alternates according to the direction of the force; b) using a compression/tension member, where the loading changes from compression to tension as the force itself changes direction; c) steel load cables can only be tension loaded. Here, too, the competence of the one or the other cable changes with the direction of the force.

A triangular effect can also be achieved with flat elements, diagonal boarding or by planking with timber-product boards admissible for reinforcement.

These procedures have marked timber construction design. Distinctions can be made between the timber constructions discussed below in terms of how their walls are reinforced. Diagonal bracing is most clearly visible in historic timber-frame buildings, but a crisscross pattern of steel cables is often part of the characteristic detail of modern skeleton construction.

O **Note:** A flat section of wall or ceiling is considered statically stable as a plate if it can absorb forces on its longitudinal axis without deformation. Resistance to the same transverse forces is considerably less, and transverse deflection results. The component is then loaded as a panel. The direction of the force applied decides whether a flat construction element functions as a plate or a panel (see Fig. 9).

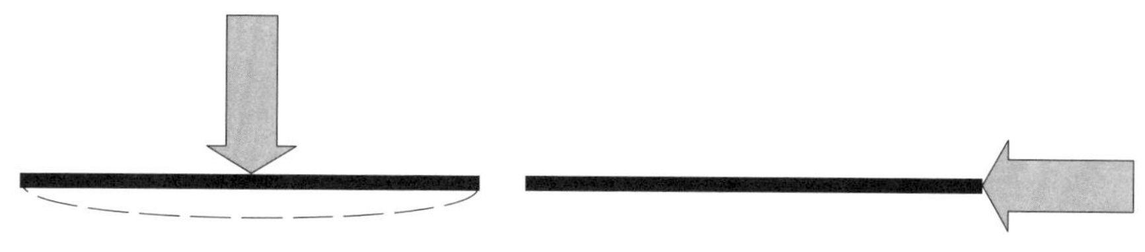

Fig. 9: Stable structure scheme (slab and disc)

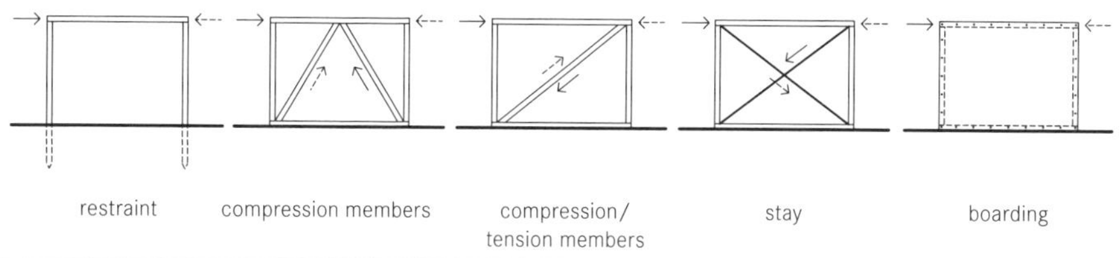

Fig.10: Wall stiffening systems

TIMBER CONSTRUCTION SYSTEMS

Building methods develop out of different conditions: climate, cultural characteristics, the availability of material, tools, and the level of craftsmanship. Stone building developed in timber-poor southern Europe, while the wooded north produced timber construction. But here, too, there are regional differences. Log construction using solid timber walls developed in the mountainous regions of the Alps and the Mittelgebirge, as well as in northern Europe with its wealth of straight-trunked conifers. In contrast, the deciduous timber prevalent in central and eastern Europe led to traditional timbered building.

In the 19th century, and particularly the 20th, new technologies and materials changed European timber construction considerably. Construction engineering developed craft joints further to create high-quality steel jointing devices that made better use of the cross section of the timbers. These were used largely in skeleton construction. In North America, rib construction established itself as timber frame building using simple nailed joints.

The timber industry is constantly putting new natural and synthetic materials on the market. New transport methods and increasing demands for thermal insulation are also contributing to the evolution of timber construction.

To this day, the history of timber building remains a story of rod-based construction principles, from log to timbered construction, from timber frame to skeleton. Hence it is essential for everyone working in the field to know and understand the systems described below, even though new systems, mainly panel-based, will expand timber construction possibilities in future.

Log construction

The term "knitted construction" (Strickbau) is also found in specialist literature, because the beams cross at the ends, so can be described as being knitted together.

One characteristic of log construction is the large amount of timber needed and the great degree of slump of the horizontally placed members. Straight softwood that has grown very regularly is the most suitable. The walls were originally constructed from round trunks, slightly levelled off at the contact surfaces. The joints between the trunks were sealed with moss, hemp or wool.

The timbers are scarf-jointed at the corners and at the tying transverse walls, and generally anchored by cogging to make them tensionproof. The beams are offset to each other by half their height. This cogged link creates a kind of bond between the two walls. > Fig. 11

The degree of craftsmanship was also enhanced by the quality of the tools. Mortise and tenon improved jointing. Using squared rather than round timber evened out the cross section of the wall. Today's beams are elaborately profiled. > Fig. 12

Joints

Typical timber construction joints are mortise and tenon between the horizontal trunks; scarf and cogging for binding walls at the corners of the building; and tensionproof dovetail joints for internal walls tying into the external ones. > Fig. 45, page 74 ○

A wall cross section consisting of single beams is no longer adequate for modern heating and cooling requirements. Modern log structures therefore have additional heat insulation. Ideally this is fitted on the outside, to avoid condensation. The horizontal timber look typical of log construction can then be achieved only by adding planks, which also protect thermal insulation material from weather. The timber industry now

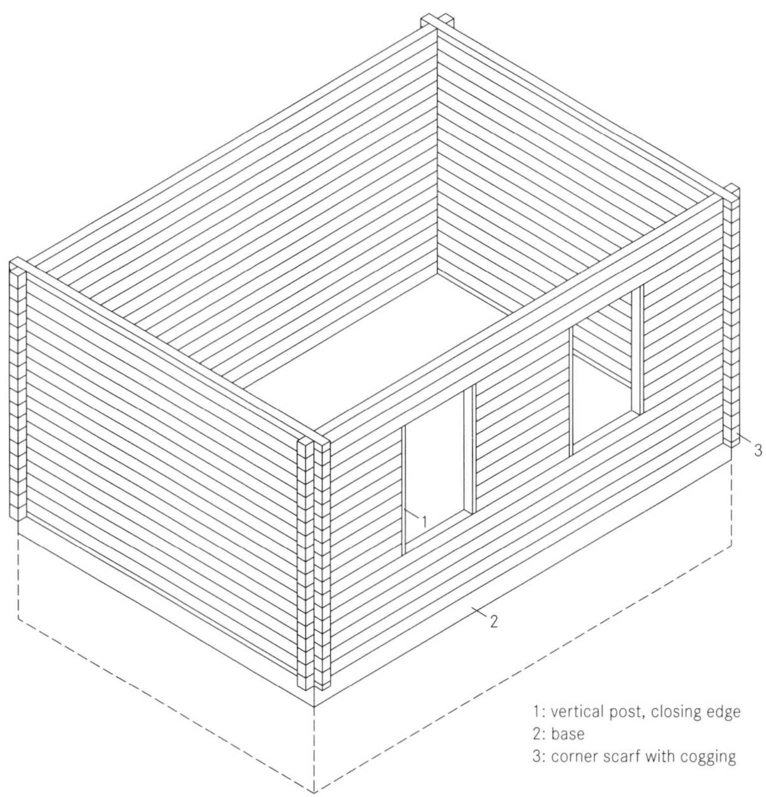

Fig.11: Isometric diagram for log construction

supplies laminated log construction wall in the form of sandwich elements of planks and insulation.

Settlement

The compression load of the beams across the grain results in a high degree of settlement for log constructions, which can be up to 2–4 cm per floor. This factor must be taken into account when making windows

> O **Note:** A scarf is a joint in which the timbers are recessed by half and fitted together flush. Tensile forces can be absorbed by additional grooving as a cogged joint. The same applies to the conical shape of a dovetail.

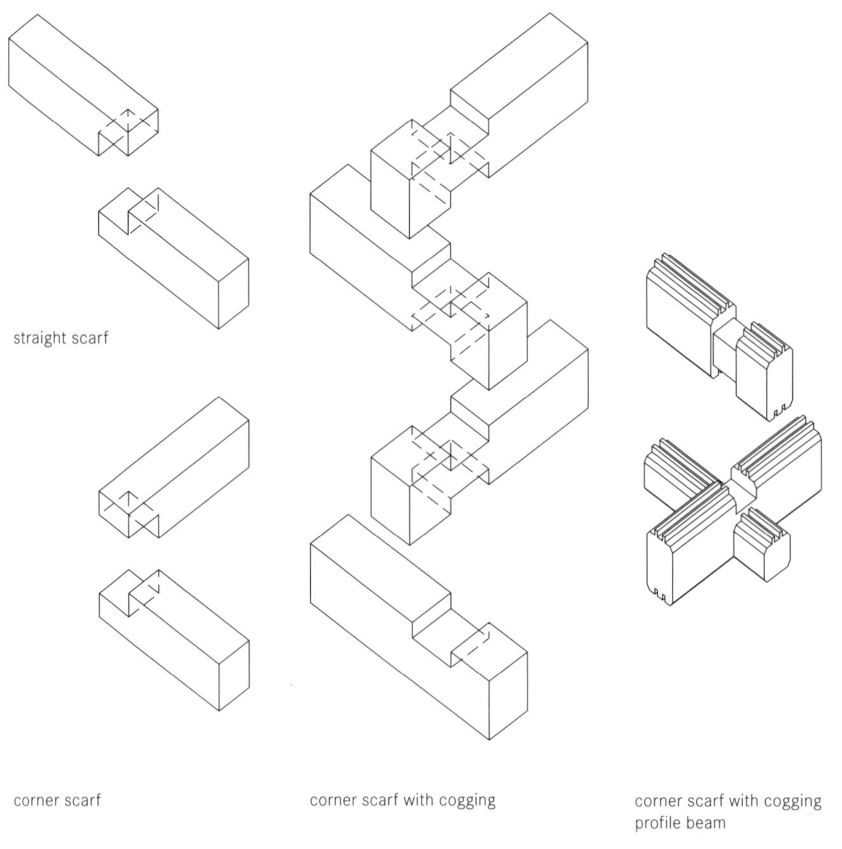

Fig. 12: Isometric scarfing diagrams, corner scarf with cogging

and doors. The vertical framework or posts are therefore recessed sufficiently at the top to absorb the settlement of the wall without creating secondary bending. > Fig. 13 Settling should also be addressed by a concealed joint between window frame and lintel. For the same reason, any vertical runs through the building (chimney or services) should not be attached to the building rigidly, but in such a way that they can move. So although log construction many look primitive at first, it does require a great deal of craftsmanship and experience.

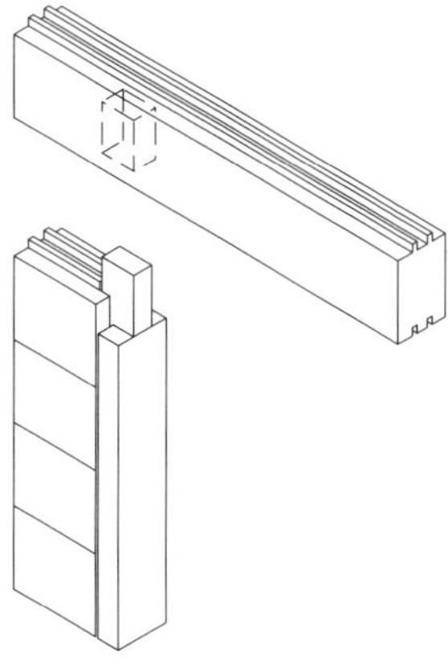

Fig. 13: Window aperture with vertical posts and settlement joint

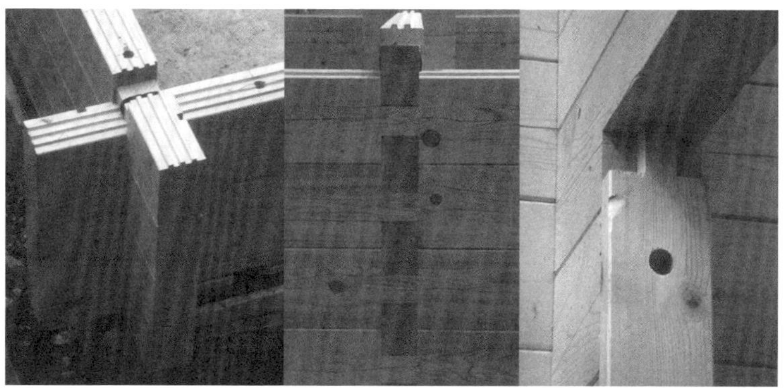

Fig. 14: Log construction – external corner, internal wall connection, window aperture

Log construction suggests a rigid, rectangular ground plan arrangement.

The facade design should ensure that any apertures are as small and few as possible, so that the wall structure is not unduly compromised. A perforated facade of the kind familiar from classical masonry structures would be the appropriate design element for log construction, which is in essence a solid construction system. > Fig. 14

Traditional timbered structures

Traditional timbered construction clearly reveals the flow of forces in the structure. For this reason German specialist publications sometimes call it the "Stil der Konstruktion" (construction style). This kind of building is particularly attractive because of the visible distinction between loadbearing and non-loadbearing parts, between structural timbers and wall elements acting as filling.

Infilling

The spaces left between the loadbearing posts are called panels or compartments. Historical timber structures are filled with masonry, or with clay and wickerwork (wattle and daub). The current demand for warm interiors makes a heat insulation infill essential, with external cladding to protect it from the weather, but needing some internal covering as well.

As the filling is not loadbearing, it is perfectly possible to make apertures in the panels of a timbered wall. Windows cannot be placed at random, but they may be numerous provided they conform to the construction grid. Thus it is easier to provide daylight for rooms in timbered buildings than in log structures.

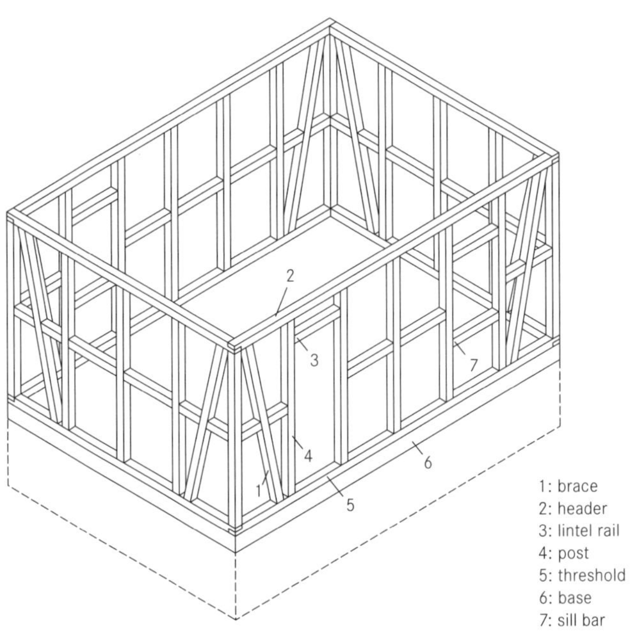

Fig. 15: Isometric drawing of a traditional timbered structure

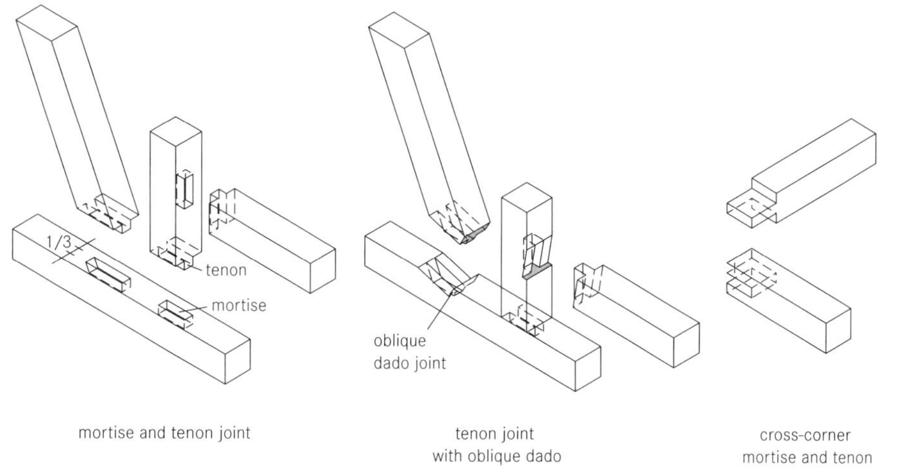

Fig. 16: Isometric diagram of mortise and tenon joint, oblique dado joint

Typical timbered construction joints are mortise and tenon, used to join timbers flush. An oblique dado joint is often used as well, to transfer forces better. Horizontal thresholds and headers are also joined by mortise and tenon or with a corner scarf. > Fig. 16 and Chapter Construction, Log construction ○

Joints

One characteristic feature of timbered structures is that the vertical posts, horizontal rails and diagonal braces are held together at the bottom by the threshold and at the top by a header. As the timbers are mainly compression loaded, square cross sections with dimensions of 10/10, 12/12 or 14/14 cm are the norm. Horizontal rectangular cross sections are often used for thresholds and headers.

Cross sections

There are also timbered structures that run through one or more floors. As horizontal timbers are used only for the threshold and header, the degree of settlement is considerably reduced; it is in any case much less than in log construction.

○ **Note:** For a tenon joint the timbers are notched by division into thirds so that mortise and tenon fit together. The mortise should be less than 4 cm deep, so that the loadbearing timber cross sections are not weakened unduly.

Ceiling The ceiling beams are placed on the header and can be seen outside through the beam ends in unclad timbered structures. The timbers for the next floor are then built on top of this, starting with the threshold. For timbered structures whose loadbearing structure runs through two or more floors, the ceiling must be suspended between the walls. > Fig. 50, page 79

Historic timbered structures are constructed from hardwood, preferably oak. Construction methods vary from region to region. In Germany a distinction is made between Franconian, Alemanic and Saxon timbered structures, for example. The structural components often differ from region to region as well, and have different names.

Grid The unit spacing between the posts is usually 100–120 cm. However, the history of timbered construction includes smaller and also considerably larger unit spacings. Despite all the structural constraints, timbered building has opened up a large number of creative possibilities in terms of both construction and design. Monument protection authorities try to secure the formal variety of historic timbered buildings and maintain their presence in the townscape. So when building within existing stock it is essential that architects be familiar with the principles of historic timbered construction. In modern timber frame building, the numerous posts, braces and rails raise the problem of filling a large number of joints with thermal insulation material, which creates a great deal of work. Nowadays the high level of manual craft input for timber jointing has largely been replaced by computer milling.

Timber frame construction

Modern timber frame construction originated in North America. Rapid settlement of the country along the new railroads demanded a simple, economical building method that could be carried out in a short time. Timber was the material that was available and suited to all the continent's different climatic conditions.

Industrial techniques started to influence timber construction in the first half of the 19th century. Steam-powered sawmills and machine-cut nails changed timber construction, which had until then been derived from traditional European timbered buildings.

Large numbers of different timber cross sections were replaced by uniform, plank-like cross sections. Simple nailed joints, easy to execute without special tools in an easy, do-it-yourself process, took over from elaborate manual jointing. The slender timber cross sections were nailed together laterally. The framework, more closely structured than in traditional timbered building, rose through the full height of the building. The

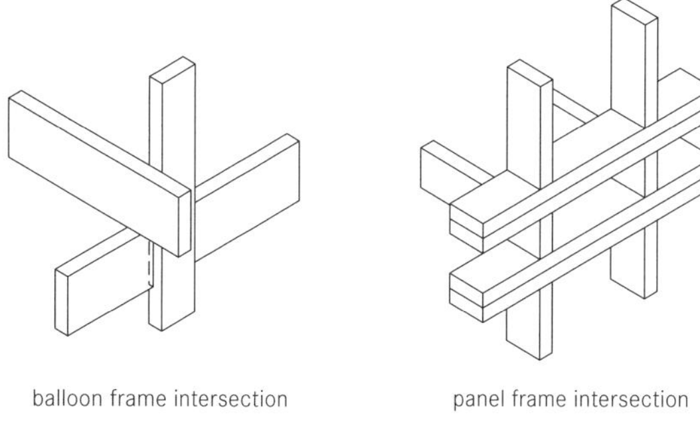

Fig.17: Isometric diagram of post-and-beam – timber-frame construction

phrase "balloon frame" was first coined as a derisive term for the unusual lightness of the structure.

This building technique was known as post-and-beam construction in Europe. The disadvantages of post-and-beam construction, the difficulty of obtaining the timber, the additional difficulties caused by placing the high structural elements in position, and also problems with sound transmitted by the vertical members running through all the storeys, led to construction floor by floor, known as "platform framing" in America. The floor slab or ceiling then served as a working platform on which to assemble the framework.

Timber frame building developed from "balloon-frame" or post-and-beam construction. This is understood as a building method using wall elements assembled as frames while still lying on the ground. The frames are usually one storey high, although there are examples of two-storey timber frames.

Rib construction

All these construction techniques are sometimes collectively called rib construction, particularly in Germany (Rippenbau) because the upright members are so close together, and because of the narrow, plank-like cross sections.

Cross sections

Modern European architecture of the early 20th century was mainly focused on concrete as a material. Timber frame construction did not therefore become widely accepted until the 1980s, when American timber construction was remembered in the search for more reasonably priced building methods. The American standard "two by four" inches

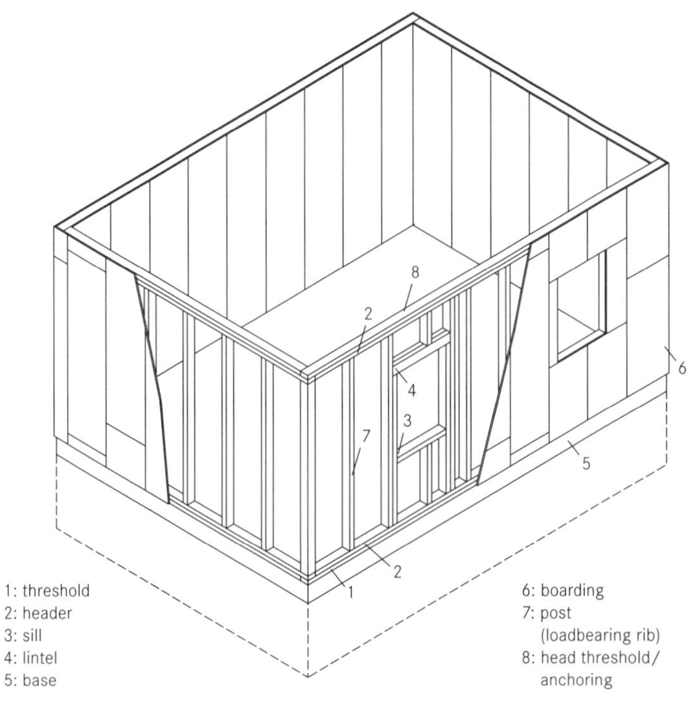

Fig. 18: Isometric diagram of timber frame construction

became 6 × 12 cm in Europe and, and thus produced somewhat sturdier timber cross sections than the American dimensions, which work out at about 5 × 10 cm. ○

Joints

Typical wood jointing for the timber frame construction method is a nailed butted joint for the timbers. Diagonal nailing is intended to create the maximum bond across the grain direction in the transverse joint. It

○ **Note:** "Two by four" (inches) is a tried-and-tested cross section for timber construction and can be used and combined in a variety of ways. Sometimes "two by four" is used as a generic term for timber frame construction as such. The higher insulation standard in the central European climate usually means that the cross section is thicker today, more like a side ratio of "two by six".

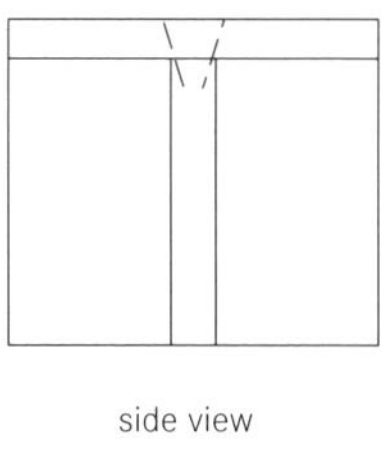

side view

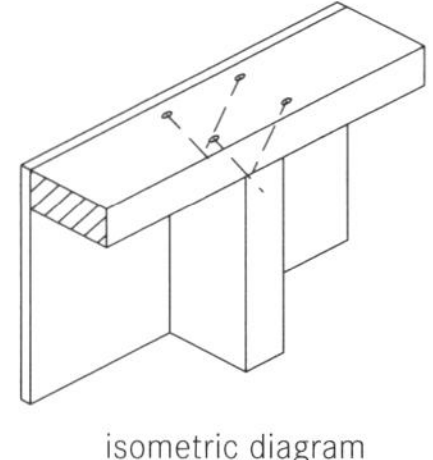

isometric diagram

Fig. 19: Nailing a butted joint

is only the timber-product panel planking that makes the joint rigid and protects the nails from being pulled out. > Fig. 19

Grid

The tight rib spacing in timber frame construction with its small grid is usually matched to the width of the panels for the stiffening panelling. A popular unit spacing is 62.5 cm. > Chapter Construction, Timber-based products Standard widths for insulation material could also be the deciding factor when dimensioning the construction grid.

One characteristic feature of timber frame construction is that the overall length of a building does not have to relate strictly to multiples of the unit spacing. The repeating pattern > Fig. 20 of the construction grid is often abandoned at the end of a wall and concluded with a special unit dimension. The arrangement of the windows and tailing internal walls can be handled freely as well; their positions are determined solely by the design and not by the construction grid, as would be the case for traditional timbered building. The construction grid in timber frame construction aims principally at using materials economically, rather than with structural and aesthetic order. Thus in comparison with other timber construction systems there are scarcely any restrictions on designing the ground plan or sections of the building.

Assembly

At the assembly stage, the structural timbers are no longer fitted together upright, as in traditional timbered building, but nailed together on the ground to form a frame, and subsequently set up on the threshold, which is firmly anchored to the floor slab, and fixed with nails. The double threshold made up of threshold and frame timbers is a typical feature of timber frame building, which uses lateral connections rather than complicated timber jointing, in other words prefers doubling or even tripling the cross sections where necessary. > Fig. 21

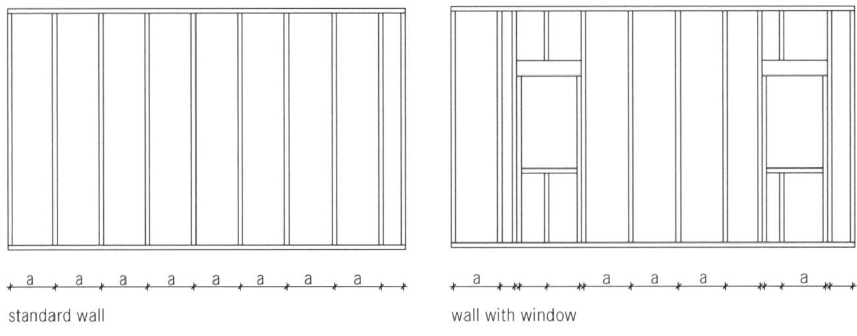

Fig. 20: View of standard wall – wall with window

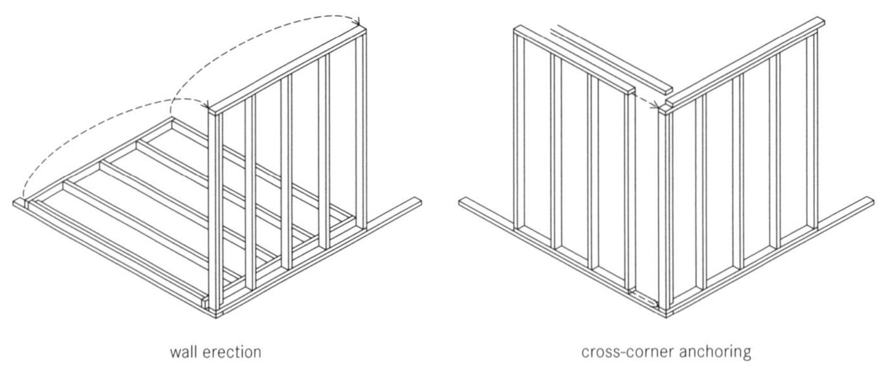

Fig. 21: Isometric diagram of wall erection – cross-corner anchoring

Walls that have been set up in this way are anchored on the same principle. The upper frames of the walls are fixed together using a second framing timber; the head threshold, which spans from one wall to the other, by a peripheral tie beam, which makes the structure tensionproof.

Ceiling

The course of beams then laid on the timber frame walls in the next step also consists of slender cross sections that correspond to the span of the ceiling. The beams are nailed to a set of beams of the same height running round the edge of the ceiling, and thus prevented from tilting. This joint is not fully stable until the ceiling is planked with timber-product panels. The timber beam ceiling thus forms a rigid plate, and can

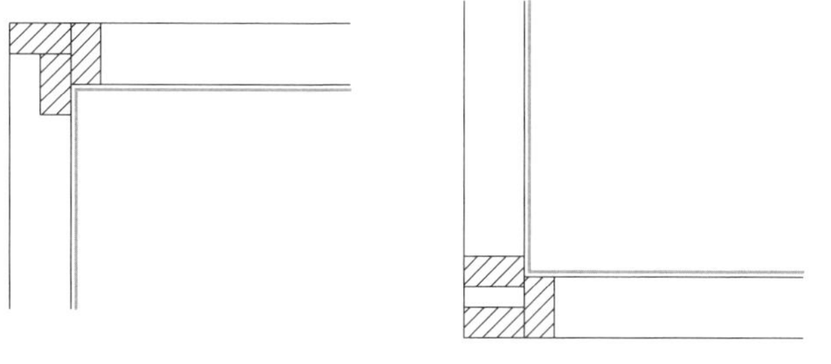

Fig. 22: Isometric diagram of corner solutions

Fig. 23: Timber frame wall – interior and exterior view

immediately be used as a platform for the next floor, whose walls are set up using the same procedure. > Fig. 21 In America, buildings can be erected up to a height of six storeys by platform framing. ○

○ **Note:** When attaching walls, the corner posts must be placed so that there is support available in both directions for fixing the inner cladding for half the width of the cross section, i.e. 3 cm. Possible solutions are shown in Fig. 22.

Skeleton construction

Skeleton construction developed from timbered construction because of a desire for more freedom in dividing up space, and for larger areas of glazing. The term skeleton construction is occasionally used for timber construction in general.

In the main, specialist literature defines a building method as skeleton construction if it is based on a primary loadbearing structure made up of columns and beams supporting a secondary loadbearing structure of beams and rafters. The walls forming a room are erected independently of the loadbearing skeleton. This makes it possible to include large areas of facade glazing, as well as allowing greater flexibility in ground plan design. Timber skeleton construction realizes the 20th century Modernist principle of "skin and skeleton".

Grid

The spaces between the loadbearing posts are considerably larger than in timber frame construction, but also larger than in traditional timbered structures. The loadbearing skeleton usually remains visible inside or outside. Glued laminated timber plays an important part in skeleton

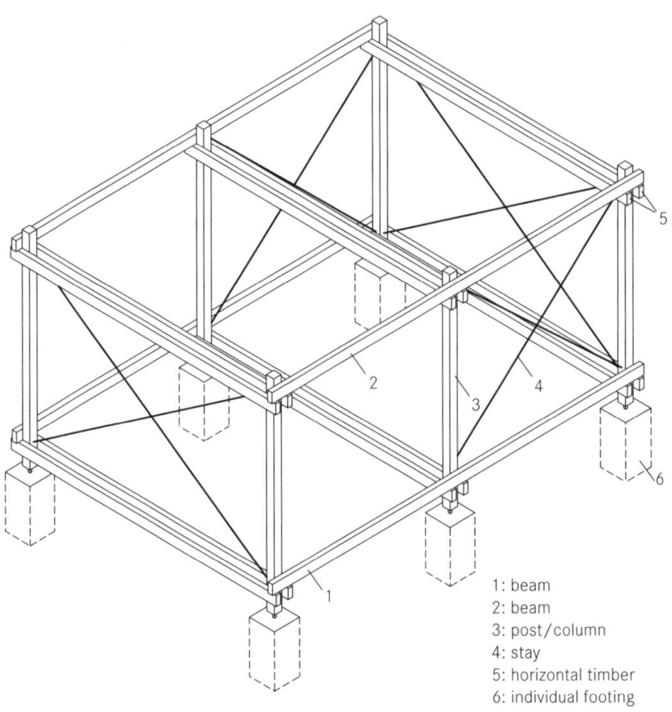

Fig. 24: Isometric diagram of skeleton construction (tie beam joints)

construction, as beams made of this make the large support spacings possible. > Chapter Building material, Timber construction products

Wind forces are usually absorbed by steel cables or round steel bars arranged crosswise, as they can take only tensile forces > Chapter Construction, Reinforcement

The wide column spacing suggests foundations based on individual footings. As the column is usually independent of the wall, the support base is not clad, so its galvanized steel joint with the footing is a striking architectural detail in the timber skeleton structure.

For buildings with more than one storey, erection is not floor by floor, but uses continuous posts. The horizontal beams are either attached in two parts as tie beams > Figs. 24 and 25, or in one part with a butted joint. > Figs. 26 and 27

Joints

In skeleton construction the columns and beams are jointed with metal devices without particularly weakening the timber cross sections. Unlike the craft joints used for log and traditional timbered construction, they are dimensioned by the structural engineers on the basis of technical construction tables. They are thus known as engineered connections.

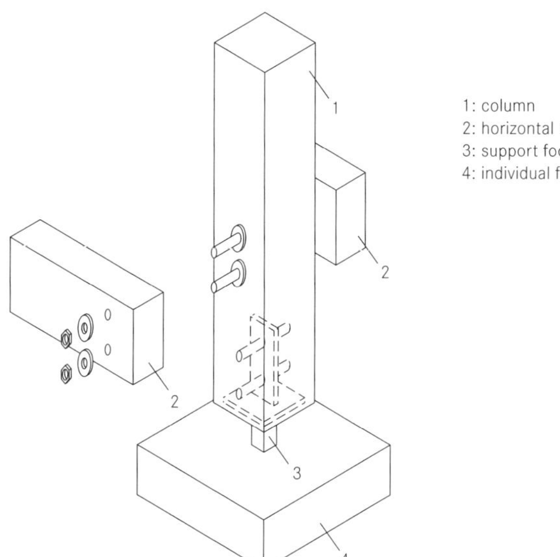

Fig. 25: Isometric diagram of a support base with dowel joints

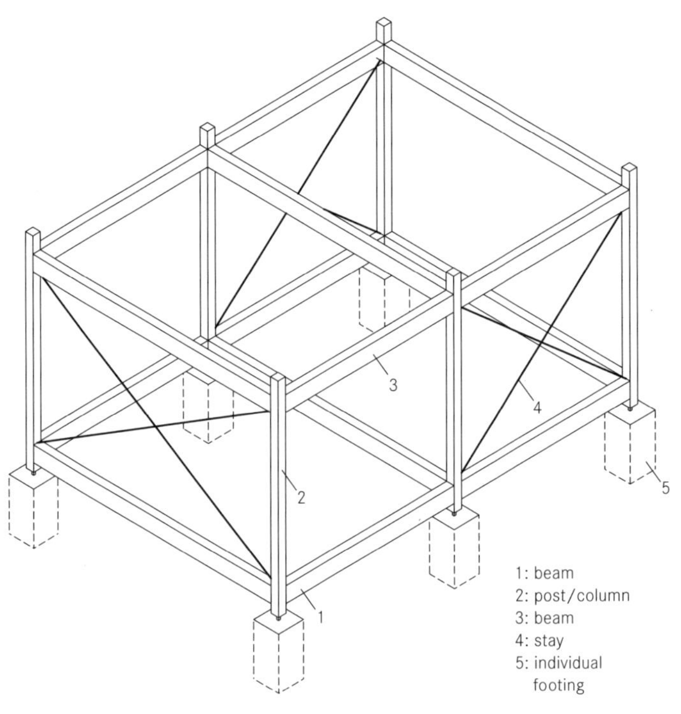

Fig. 26: Isometric diagram of skeleton construction (butted joint)

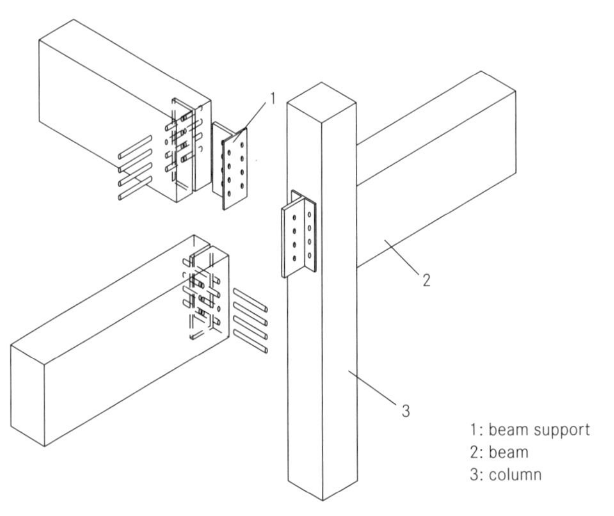

Fig. 27: Isometric diagram of a butted beam-column joint

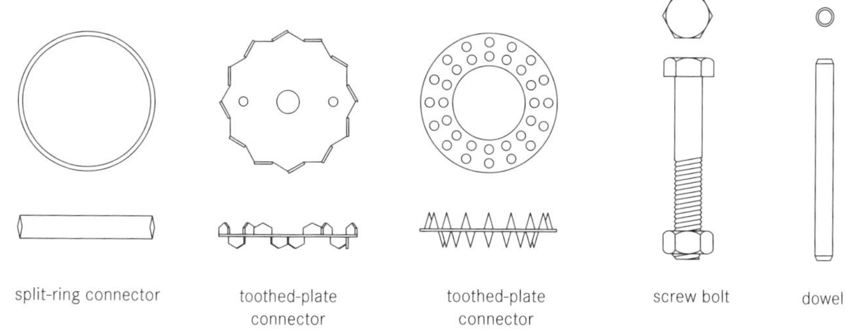

Fig. 28: Specially designed connectors, screw bolts, dowel

Jointing materials

So that forces can be transmitted more effectively when timber components are joined laterally, > Fig. 25, specially designed connectors > Fig. 28 are usually inserted in a ring shape or driven in; these take the loads from the forces acting on the joint and transfer them to the maximum number of timber fibres. The joints are held together with screwed bolts.

Another kind of connector is the round steel dowel, which is driven into pre-drilled holes and transfers the load in association with steel plates that are mortised into the timber. In butted joints this means a connection can be made between beam and column that is largely invisible from the outside. > Fig. 27, Fig. 50, page 79, and Chapter Components, Ceilings

Timber panel construction

The particular advantages of timber construction include relatively short assembly times and the dry construction system, which means that the completed structure can be occupied immediately. This short building period is considerably reinforced by the extent to which individual components, wall elements or entire room cells are prefabricated in the workshop.

Prefabrication

Timber frame building with its frame-like walls is particularly suited to prefabrication in the carpenter's workshop. Efforts to shift the maximum number of production phases from the building site to the workshop make the building process independent of weather conditions.

Timber panel construction maximizes this approach. The prefabricated panel units, usually a full storey high, are insulated and fitted with all the layers of building components and the external and internal cladding, so that on site they have only to be erected and fixed together. One

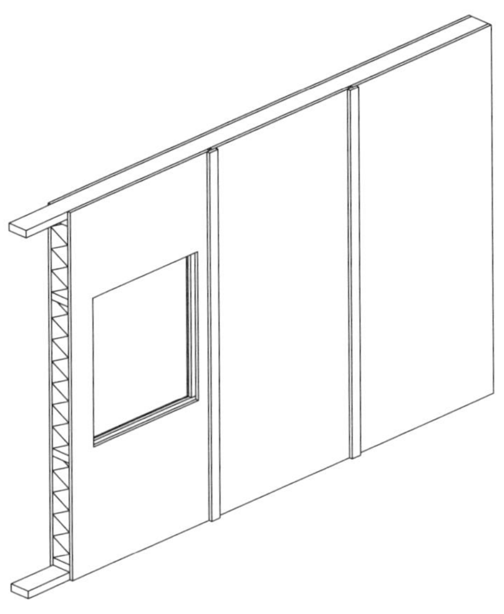

Fig. 29: Timber panel unit

essential detail is the jointing or unit butting. The floor and ceiling panels are also prefabricated and either placed on the wall units or suspended between them.

Timber panel building as a basic panel construction approach still requires a relatively large proportion of manual craftsmanship. But in recent years there has been a trend towards industrialization. Loadbearing wall units in solid cross-laminated plywood or edge-glued elements rather like oversized timber-product panels are produced by the timber industry for panel construction. It could almost be called slab construction.

This means that timber construction is increasingly turning away from stave to solid construction. For decades the rule was that the raw material wood should be used as sparingly as possible for timber construction. There now seems to be a change of direction, heralded by industrial building methods and a more consistent use of the raw material. > Chapter Construction, Timber-based products

Slab construction

Slab construction using concrete panels is familiar from the Eastern European countries and Scandinavia. Because the concrete slabs are so heavy, unit size was restricted to a single storey. Timber is light in com-

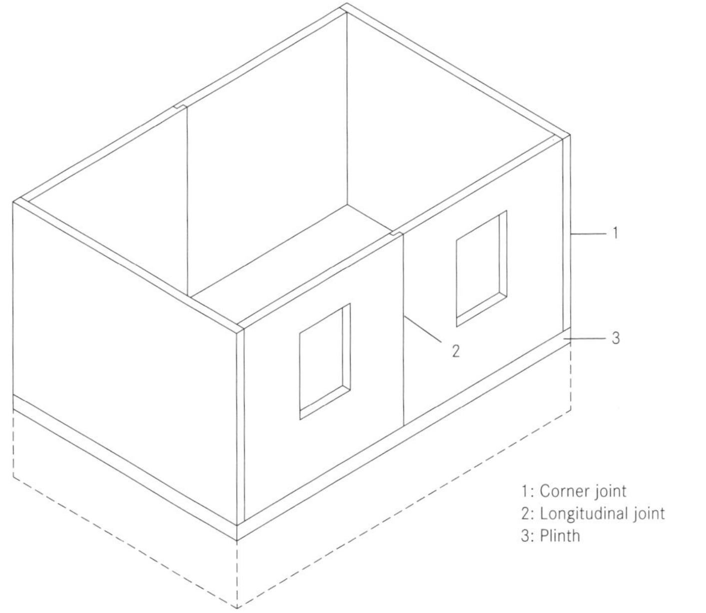

Fig. 30: Isometric of solid panel construction

parison, and permits units up to four storeys high. It is also possible to produce units to order, thus avoiding the danger of unduly stereotypical architecture, which is a general problem of prefabricated and unified facade units. Such production is made easier by CAD and computer-controlled machines.

Whether this slab construction method will become more generally accepted than stave construction for timber depends on various economic factors. Higher wage costs for stave construction have to be set against the disadvantage of elaborate and costly lifting devices, greater transport difficulties and large production shops.

Solid panel construction

For construction methods using solid timber panels, we can find the term "solid panel construction" in the literature. The basic material used to produce these solid timber panels consists of boards or planks that are joined into solid panels, either by gluing them together to form glue-laminated timber using edge-glued construction, or by cross-laminating them to produce cross-laminated timber. Another option is to nail planks together side by side in the upright position to produce nail-laminated timber elements.

In addition there are special inventions, for example walls consisting of vertical planks, which are joined together in several layers without glue or metal, simply using a type of dovetail key. This requires a high degree of precision, which can be achieved with CNC machining. All these construction systems have the benefit that no shrinkage and hence no settling takes place.

For our purpose here we want to focus on cross-laminated timber, which is often used in construction. In this type of panel construction, construction grids such as those used in half-timbered construction, in timber framing, and in skeleton construction are no longer relevant. This means that there is greater design freedom, because the panel sizes can be determined to suit the respective design and layout. However, structural dimensions are determined by the structural design, taking into account structural stability, spans, buckling lengths, and bracing of the building.

Loadbearing cross-laminated timber walls are at least one story high, but can often also extend through two or more stories; they are used in combination with solid deck panels to join the structure. The height of the elements is largely determined by the limitations of transport as well as by the available space at the workshop.

The degree of prefabrication can vary. At the basic level, shell construction elements without insulation are used with all openings already in place. At the more sophisticated level, wall elements are delivered to the site with insulated and clad surfaces, and including windows and doors. In some instances prefabrication involves the construction of entire three-dimensional room modules. Whatever the degree of prefabrication, construction time is reduced and much of the work takes place in the workshop.

The loadbearing components are panels consisting of cross-laminated timber, similar to plywood in furniture construction. Whereas in furniture construction the plywood consists of an uneven number of millimeter-thin layers of veneer glued crosswise > Chapter Timber-based products, cross-laminated timber consists of boards laminated to form wall thicknesses of between 5 and 30 cm, which results in a high degree of rigidity and strength.

Jointing

The wall elements are screwed together at the corners of the building or where internal walls butt up to external walls; screws are inserted at vertical intervals of up to 30 cm. In view of the fact that the layers of board have different orientations, the screw fixing needs to follow the

Fig. 31: Photo of solid panel construction

same rules as those used for fixing into end-grain. Since no adequate tensile strength can be achieved by inserting a screw head-on into the end-grain, it is necessary to insert the fasteners from two sides at an angle. Depending on the thickness of the panels, the screws can be fastened using angles of up to 45°. > Fig. 32

Cross connectors

Another option for joining end-grain timber is to use steel bolt connectors, such as those used in furniture construction.

In this method a steel cylinder or half-cylinder is inserted into a precisely dimensioned hole; this can be turned with the help of a screwdriver so that the threaded hole is exactly in line with the connecting bolt, which is then turned into the cylinder. In this way the tensile forces are evenly transferred to the timber fibers via the entire length of the steel cylinder. > Fig. 34

The corner connections can either involve a butt or a rebated joint. Joints within internal walls are generally butt joints. > Fig. 33 In addition to these cross connections, it is usually also necessary to join timbers longitudinally; the joint used for this purpose is a lap joint. > Chapter Log construction In this connection the screws are inserted perpendicular to the grain, which results in a structurally effective joint.

Floor decks

The type of connection for the floor decks is determined by the height of the wall elements. In the case of story-high elements, the solid floor panel can be placed and screwed directly on to the wall, covering its full thickness. As in timber frame construction, the wall of the next story is placed on to the floor panel and fastened using steel angles. > Chapter Ceilings

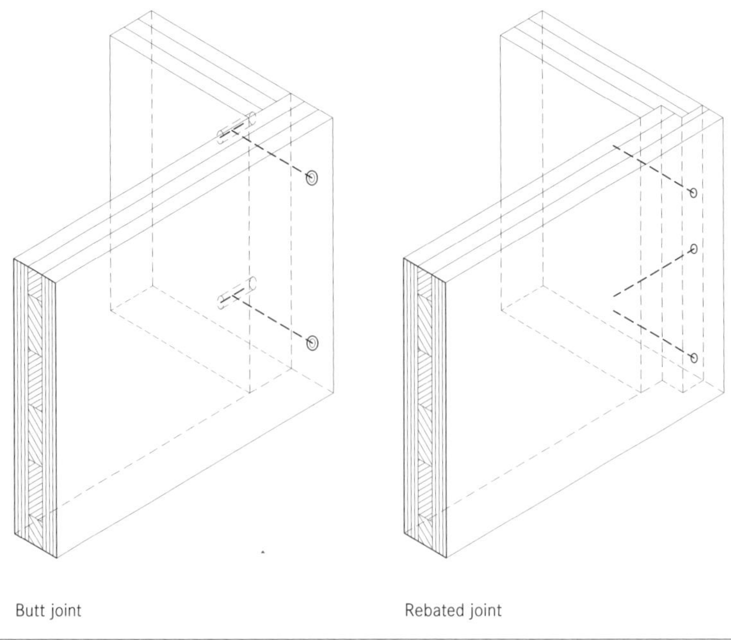

Fig. 32: Isometric of corner joints

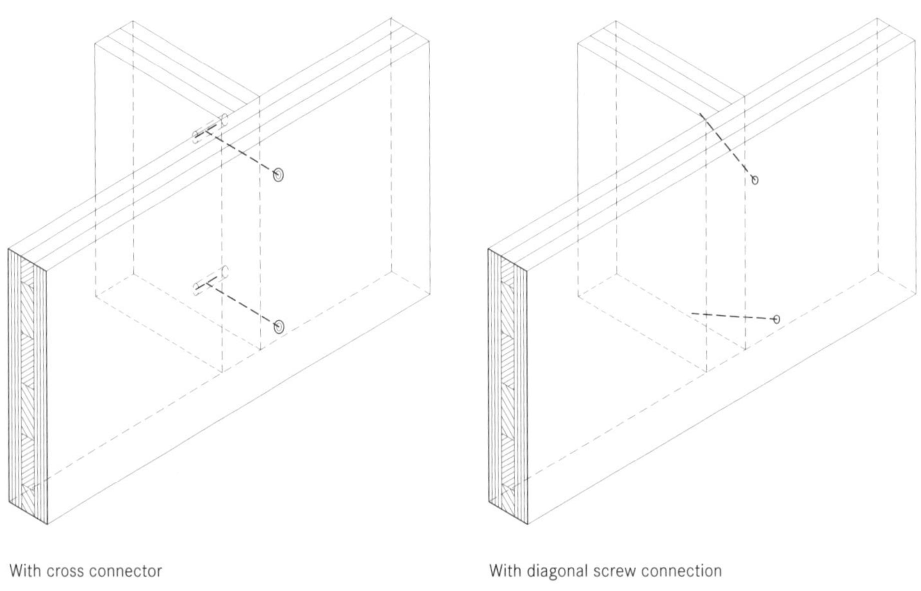

Fig. 33: Isometric of internal wall connection

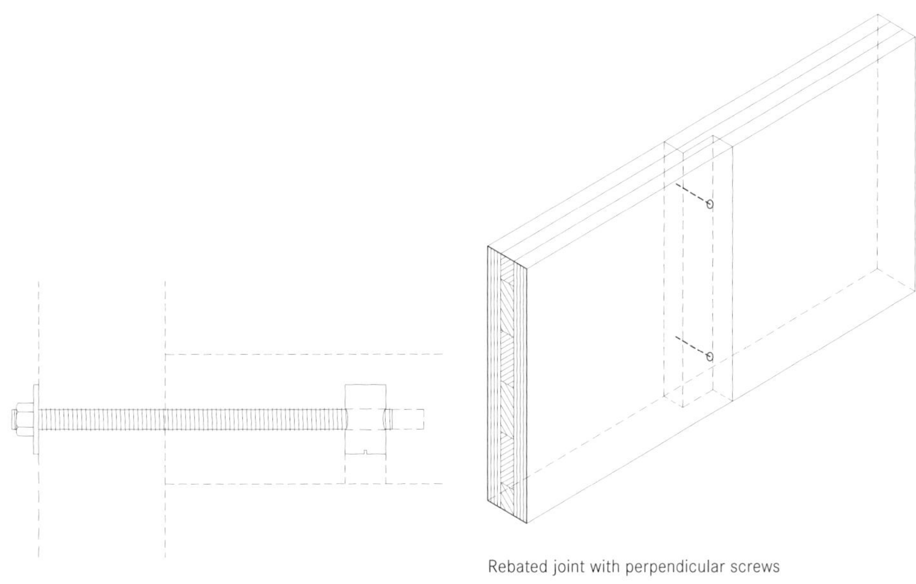

Fig. 34: Bolt connector diagram

Fig. 35: Isometric of longitudinal joint

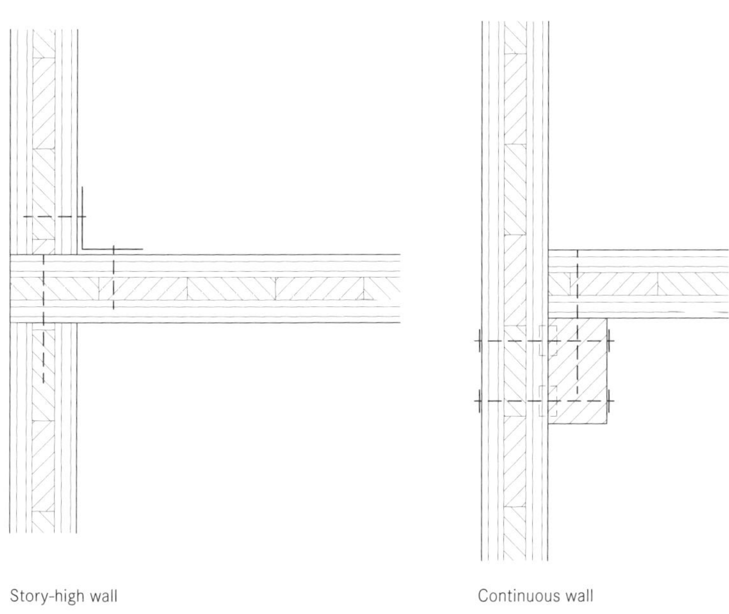

Fig. 36: Section through floor bearing

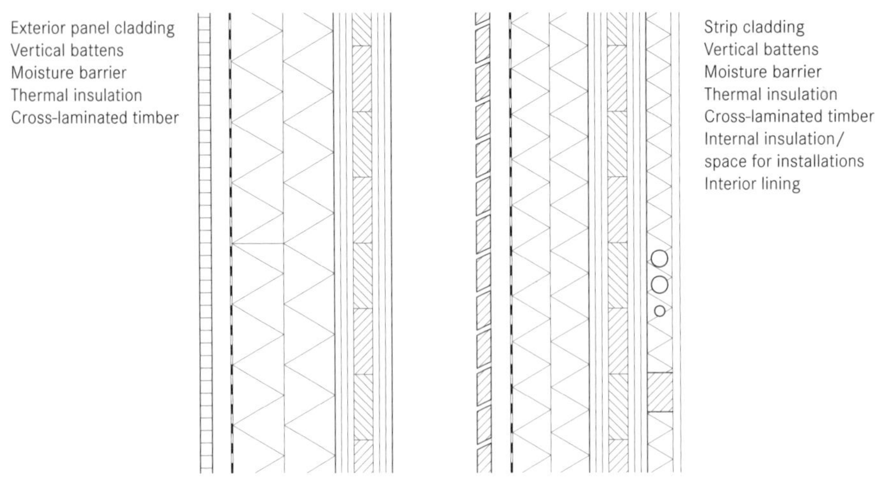

Fig. 37: Section through wall construction

In the case of wall elements extending through two or several stories, it is necessary to attach a bearing beam or a continuous steel profile, either angled or U-shaped, to the walls as a bearing for the floor panel.

Wall construction

Flat roofs are constructed in a similar manner. In the case of a sloping roof it is possible to construct a conventional roof structure on top of the last floor panel or to use solid timber panels for the sloping roof surfaces, in line with the construction method of the building.

Even though there are some timber construction systems that work without external insulation and instead use solid timber of adequate thickness, it is more common in solid panel construction that the panel elements only form the shell building and, in addition, thermal insulation and an external skin are applied. The principle of this wall construction is similar to that used in modern masonry block construction. The insulation is typically fitted on the outside for reasons of building physics and can be finished off with a facade consisting of panel materials or timber boarding; as these are open to the elements, a moisture barrier is also needed to protect the insulation. > Chapter External wall Using screws of appropriate length it is possible to fasten the supporting battens directly to the cross-laminated timber elements. In principle it is also possible to use a composite thermal insulation system with a render finish, especially since no deformation due to shrinkage or swelling is likely to occur in cross-laminated timber. It is generally not necessary to fit a vapor barrier on the inside of the wall, which means that the interior finish will be largely determined by the interior design. However, in many cases an interior installation layer is needed, which also provides space for additional thermal insulation. In this case, this layer needs to be finished with plasterboard or wood-based panels.

Foundations

The foundations for these systems are not significantly different to those for other timber construction systems. The solid panel walls are either placed on to a reinforced concrete floor slab or on a horizontal floor panel that is supported on strip foundations. The floor panel then supports the entire solid panel structure. It goes without saying that the rules of structural timber protection also apply to solid panel construction. This means that it is best to use a concrete base and plinth on which the building is placed on the site.

Range of systems

Timber construction offers a relatively wide range of construction systems. The choice of construction system for a particular design depends on a number of factors. At one level, a decision has to be made as to whether to opt for an open or closed construction system, i.e. for skeleton or solid construction. In addition the choice of system is also affected by structural considerations and by the constraints of manufacturing, transport, and installation.

In spite of these many options, however, development in timber construction is still ongoing. In a fairly recent development, timber is also being used in combination with other materials, e.g. reinforced concrete, in a hybrid design. This is intended to make the best possible use of both timber and reinforced concrete by combining the two materials.

Components

This third section of the book addresses the essential points of detail for base, wall, ceiling and roof, and the way they are integrated into the overall timber construction pattern. Particular attention will be paid to the relatively complicated layer structure and to connections and junctions with adjacent building components. ○

Each of the building components is illustrated with detailed examples of solutions on a scale of 1:10 as timber frame or traditional timbered structures. These demonstrate contexts and problems, without claiming to come anywhere near covering the enormous range of possible detail.

FOUNDATIONS

As structural timber has to be protected, the foundations of any timber structure should raise it about 30 cm above the ground. The timber structure stands either on the ceiling of the cellar, or if there are no cellars, directly on a concrete or masonry foundation. Provided that the nature of the subsoil does not dictate special foundations, there are three basic foundation types available for timber construction: > Fig. 38

- Slab foundations = flat
- Strip foundations = linear
- Individual footing = point

Slab foundations

Any timber construction system can use a foundation slab. Slab foundations are particularly appropriate for timber frame construction, which needs a platform to work on for assembly. The concrete floor slab can float either on a layer of compacted frost blanket gravel (coarse gravel) or on a continuous ice wall taken down to the frost line.

○ **Note:** This book will address roof construction and structures on roofs only to the extent necessary for external wall junctions, as roofs are dealt with in the separate volume *Basics Roof Construction* by Ann-Christin Siegemund, Birkhäuser.

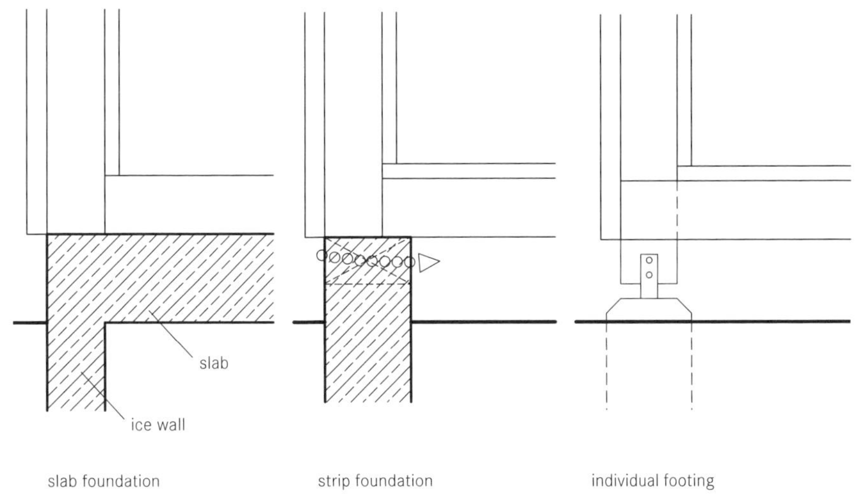

Fig. 38: Schemes for slab foundation – strip foundation – individual footing

If there are cellars under the building, the cellar ceiling, usually made of reinforced concrete, replaces the foundation slab.

Strip foundations

If strip foundations are used a special floor structure must be made of timber planks. The crucial factor here is structural timber protection, which requires ventilation under the floor structure. The space between the ground and the wooden joists must be closed so that it is not accessible to small animals, but adequate cross-ventilation must also be ensured to keep air flowing around the timber joists.

Another important point is that thermal insulation is required for this type of foundation. After the timbers have been laid on the strip foundations the heat insulation can be inserted between the joists from above only. First, boards must be fixed on battens, which have previously been attached to the sides of the joists. > Fig. 41, page 60 One alternative to this building method would be to lay prefabricated insulated ceiling units.

In both cases the joists are dimensioned similarly to a normal floor unit, according to the size of the open span over the strip foundations > Chapter Components, Ceilings

Individual footings

Individual footings are a foundation type particularly suited to skeleton construction. The building loads are concentrated on very few columns in skeleton construction, and are transferred to the subsoil at particular points. This reduces foundation excavations to a minimum.

The floor is structured similarly to the intermediate floors, usually with main and subsidiary joists for skeleton construction.

For reasons of structural timber protection, the industry provides various shaped parts in galvanized steel for the transition from column to foundations, > Fig. 39 the point at which the wooden column meets the concrete foundations. Despite this, particular attention must be paid at this sensitive point to keeping the support base as freely ventilated as possible and to allowing precipitation water to run off the timber unimpeded. > Chapter Building material, Timber protection

Base

Particular demands are made on the base zone of a building regardless of the construction method. They are caused by moisture from the ground, spray from precipitation or snow in winter. For reasons of structural timber protection, > Chapter Building material, Timber protection the external timber wall should be 30 cm from the ground. It is then connected to the ground with damp-resistant materials.

Constructing the base from exposed concrete is a common solution. The concrete provides protection from damp while giving the building a visible conclusion. For this reason the concrete foundation slab is

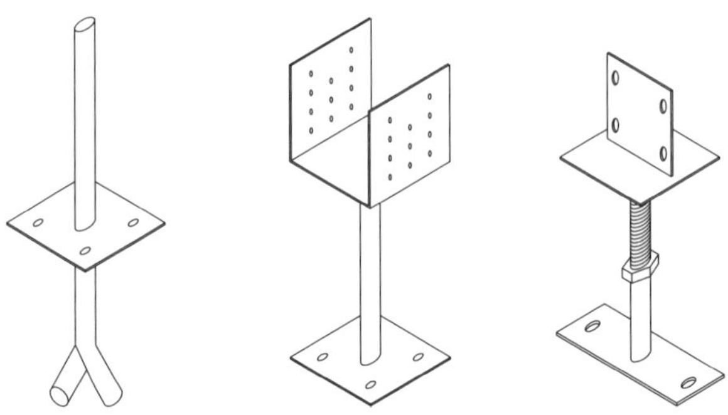

Fig. 39: Shaped steel parts for column bases

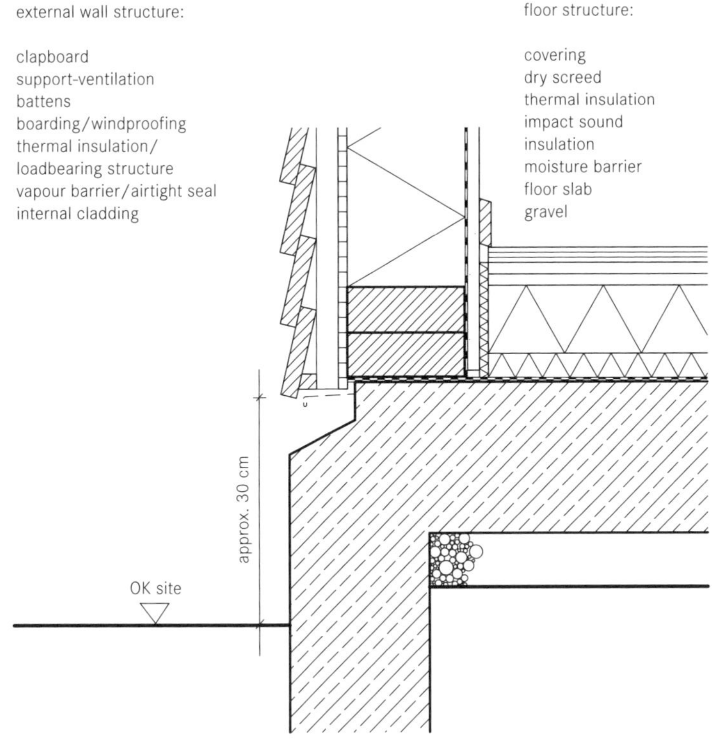

Fig. 40: Concrete slab foundation, panel base, timber frame construction

continued outwards to the facade plane. Using poured concrete, the base can be shaped so as to provide unimpeded ventilation behind the facade. To avoid ghost markings on the base surface, it should not be quite flush with the timber cladding, but very slightly recessed by the dimensions of a drip edging. The ventilated area behind the timber cladding must have an insect screen on the outside. > Fig. 40

Timber protection

Because it is so exposed and so close to the damp ground, a particularly resistant hardwood should be used as a threshold. Local legislation should be researched to determine whether it is possible to manage without chemical timber protection in this case, as would be permissible under German timber protection regulations. The timber must be separated from the damp concrete by an impervious course. The floor seal on the

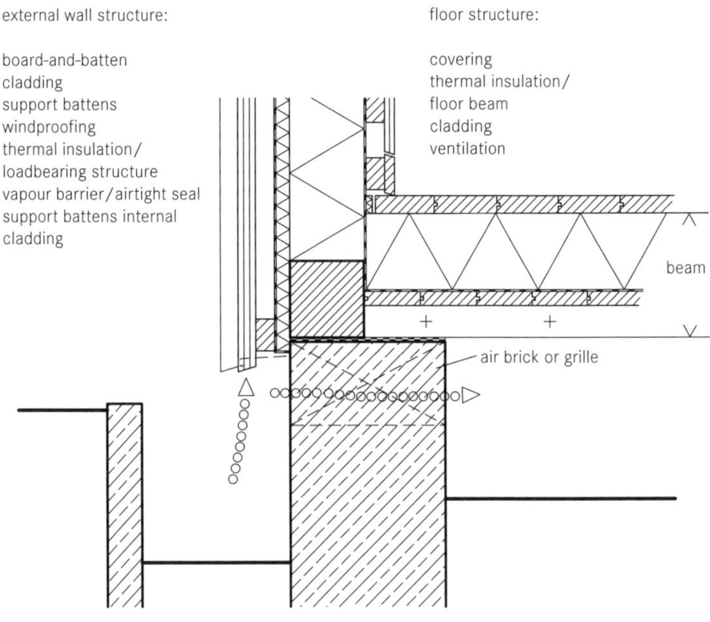

Fig. 41: Base strip foundation, timbered wall

foundation slab and the vapour barrier membrane in the external wall are brought together at this point.

Figure 41 shows a solution in which the concrete strip foundation under the external loadbearing wall forms the base. The strip foundation is so wide that it is able to support the wall threshold and the joists under the floor structure. Then a surface humidity seal is not needed, but the cavity between the timber floor and the soil must be permanently ventilated. Ventilation grids or bricks should be incorporated into the foundations to ensure cross-ventilation under the building.

O **Note:** Timber buildings must be anchored to the foundations. Both the threshold and the construction posts are attached to the floor slab or the strip foundations at regular intervals by connection anchors or heavy-duty dowels.

The visible base of the building is a key factor in determining the appearance of a timber structure. If, as in the case shown, the access height to the building is to be reduced, giving at least the impression of a building without a base, it is possible to lower the ground level in the immediate vicinity of the building. The base is set somewhat lower, in a trench running around the building, and there is still structural timber protection. For safety purposes it is best to cover this trench with a grille.

EXTERNAL WALL

As the building's envelope, the external wall has to withstand a number of stresses. It is affected from the outside by wind and rain, as well as by fluctuating temperatures, noise and radiation. From inside to outside the external wall has to contend with temperature gradient, air convection, sound transmission and water vapour diffusion.

Layered structure

In masonry construction, as well as in traditional log construction, one and the same material carries the load, insulates, seals and protects. The lightweight timber skeleton construction method distributes these tasks between various layers and specific materials. They have to be arranged in the correct sequence and matched to each other, as the system cannot accommodate omissions or weak points. The architect determines the structure, dimensions the thickness of the layers and clarifies the connections. The first decision to be made is on a single- or double-leaf structure. > Fig. 42

The fundamental difference between double- and single-leaf wall structures concerns the question of ventilation between the outer skin and the loadbearing wall. In a single-leaf structure the outer skin and the loadbearing wall together constitute a leaf; in a double-leaf structure the wall is divided into an inner and an outer leaf by the ventilation space. Each leaf has its own functions:

Outer leaf	Weatherproofing, ventilation
Inner leaf	Windproofing, thermal insulation/loadbearing structure, vapour barrier/air seal, airtightness, internal cladding

Building science

The safest, and thus also the most common version, is <u>double-leaf construction</u> with ventilation space. This space functions as an expansion chamber and provides pressure compensation for penetrating water. Care should be taken to ensure that precipitation water is able to drain away freely. At the same time the ventilation space means that water Ventilation

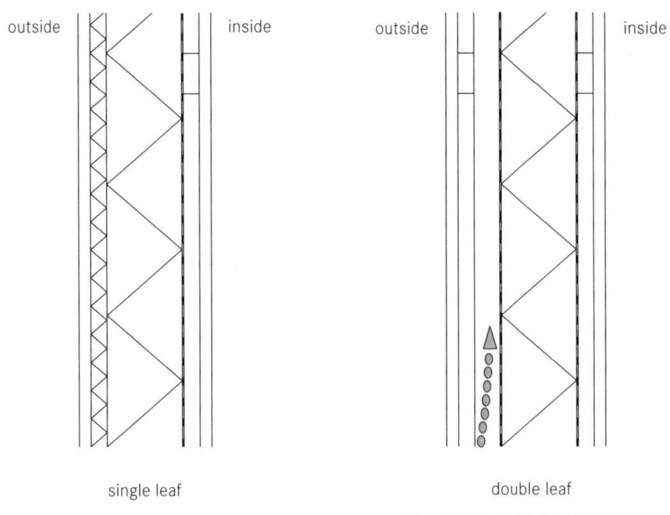

Fig. 42: Single-/double-leaf wall system

vapour from the interior of the building, or moisture from the thermal insulation, can be removed by the flow of air. Such ventilation is also advantageous in that it excludes summer heat by dispersing much of the warm air generated by the hot facade.

The ventilation space must be at least 20 mm deep, and must not be compromised by other items like windows and base. The air should come in at the base and be able to escape at the top of the wall, at the edge of the roof. The inlet and outlet apertures must be covered with an insect screen.

Windproofing

Windproofing material is applied to outside the thermal insulation. It prevents the thermal insulation from cooling off too quickly and stops air penetrating from the outside at the joints between the thermal insulation and the timber structure.

In the case of external cladding with open joints, > Chapter Components, External cladding the windproofing material must also protect the thermal insulation from damp penetration. To meet the requirement for increasing vapour permeability from the inside to the outside, the windproofing must however admit as much diffusion as possible. The timber-product stiffening panel takes over this function for structures whose loadbearing elements have stiffening boarding on the outside if the butted joints have a rebate. Otherwise films or sheeting are used.

One of the reasons why timber construction is so popular with architects and their clients is that it copes considerably better than masonry with demands made on thermal insulation and increasing efforts to save energy. Timbers 12–16 cm thick with insulating infill provide good insulation values in their own right, although additional insulating layers are usually applied inside or outside.

Thermal insulation/ loadbearing structure

Almost all the commercially available materials can be used for insulation. However, expanded and extruded polystyrene (EPS and XPS) and all rigid foam panels are problematic in that they cannot accommodate to timber shrinkage in the compartments. In this respect, fibre insulating material in the form of panels that can compensate for timber movement are better because they are easily compressed. ■

Insulation using loose-fill cellulose made of recycled paper is another common solution. It is blown in, and can be used only in closed cavities. This makes it particularly suitable for insulation in timber frame structures with closed chambers created by the posts and panelling.

Cellulose insulation absolutely must be protected from damp, as the walls could otherwise be deformed by the considerable increase in volume, causing structural damage that could be difficult to repair. Boron compounds are used to protect it against rot and high flammability.

The chapter Timber protection showed in detail that timber must be protected against damp. This applies not only to damp penetrating from the outside, but also to water vapour inside the building, which accumulates in the structure as condensation.

Vapour-/ airtightness

Moisture can penetrate parts of the building by diffusion (vapour) or convection (interior air). Thus the need to be vapour- and airtight is a key

■ **Tip:** The gaps between the loadbearing structure and the insulation can be bridged by additional internal or external insulation extending beyond the compartments. Low-density wood fibreboard panels (see Chapter Building material, Timber-based products) are often used because of their relatively good inherent stability, and they are often used for windproofing and, in the bituminized version, for protection against damp behind the external cladding as well.

factor in timber construction. Vapour barriers and airtightness provisions are intended to prevent the insulating effect being lost by condensation or draughts as a result of permeability or leaks.

This applies to both single- and double-leaf systems. An airtight envelope is required, with as few penetrations or connections as possible. The vapour barrier and airtightness functions are generally combined in a single layer, which is placed inside the thermal insulation.

Thermal diffusion resistance

In principle, the external wall should be constituted so that vapour diffusion into the component is prevented and any water vapour that may already have penetrated is removed to the outside. Care should thus be taken when installed wall materials that the thermal diffusion resistance (S_d) decreases from the inside to the outside.

We distinguish the S_d values:

Diffusible	S_d < 2 m
Vapour retarder	S_d 2–1500 m
Vapour barrier	S_d ≥ 1500 m

A vapour retarder is adequate for double-leaf construction. It is made of special paper or film and ensures that the water vapour generated within the building can diffuse to the outside, dosed and controlled by the thermal insulation, and is removed by the ventilation.

Single-leaf, unventilated structures need an internal vapour barrier. This is intended to prevent water vapour diffusing from the inside to the outside. The vapour barrier consists of vapourproof strips of plastic or metal film.

External cladding

The outer skin of timber or timber products provides weatherproofing for timber construction. But it is not uncommon to find cladding in other materials such as metal or plaster in some countries, such as America. For structural reasons alone it makes sense to combine materials with the same properties. This applies particularly to wood, which as a living material swells and shrinks. Design also thrives on the expressive quality of wood as a building material, its expressive properties, surface and texture.

Exterior cladding offers a large number of design possibilities. They include the choice of cladding type, the width of the boards or panels, their direction, the type of timber, surface treatment and patination.

The substructure of loadbearing battens is invisible, but is still an essential component of the external cladding. The type of substructure depends on whether the cladding is ventilated, and whether it runs horizontally or vertically. It is attached to the loadbearing structure. The supporting battens are spaced according to the external cladding board thicknesses and vice versa. > Tab. 8

Substructure

The principle of transverse arrangement requires horizontal loadbearing battens for vertical cladding. Here, vertical counter or ventilation battens are also required in order to guarantee uninterrupted air circulation from bottom to top, which horizontal battens would prevent. Vertical loadbearing battens fulfil this function for horizontal cladding.

Fixing

Screws, nails or brackets can be used to fix the boards. Nailing carries the risk of damage to the surface of the cladding and of the substructure. Screw fixing is safer and more readily controllable.

Corrosion-resistant materials are not necessary in every case, but nails or screws made of stainless steel or galvanized material are generally used to avoid rust marks on the surface of the wood. Fixing should be done so as to ensure that the wood is not prevented from shrinking and swelling. If cladding boards overlap, as in the case of board-and-batten or lap-joint cladding, the nails or screws have to past through one board only. Covering strips should be fixed to a single plank, or in the joint. The screwing or nailing should not pass through end-grain timber in secondary components either.

Tab.8: Batten spacings

Board thickness [mm]	Batten spacing [mm]
18	400–550
22	550–800
24	600–900
28	800–1050

○ **Note:** The S_d value of a component layer expresses its diffusion resistance as the thickness of a notional layer of air in repose with the same resistance. It is measured in metres and is the product of the thickness of the material (S) and its diffusion resistance m. $S_d = m \times S(m)$. The greater the S_d value of a layer, the more vapourtight it is.

○ **Note:** The properties and effect of timber as facade cladding are studied in greater detail in the volume *Basics Materials* by Manfred Hegger, Hans Drexler and Martin Zeumer, Birkhäuser.

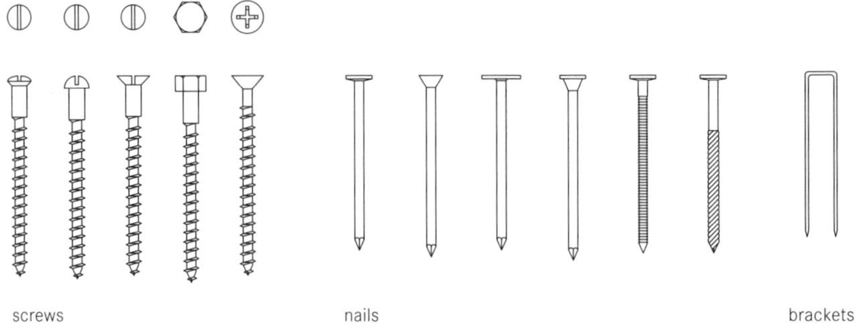

Fig. 43: Screws, nails, brackets

Vertical claddings include: > Fig. 45

- Board-and-batten cladding
- Coverstrip cladding
- Lidded cladding
- Matchboard cladding ■

Board-and-batten cladding

Floor and covering boards overlap by about 20 mm in board-and-batten cladding. Thus, when using boards of the same width, this produces a rhythmic visual impression of wide covering boards and narrower floorboards. One feature of this type is that, like coverstrip cladding, it has a relatively strongly profiled surface. ■

Coverstrip cladding

In coverstrip cladding, the gap of about 10 mm between the vertical cladding boards is covered by a strip in order to prevent penetration by precipitation water. > Figs. 44 and 45

Lidded cladding

The finishing strip is on the inside in lidded cladding, producing a relatively smooth, flush outer skin, as in matchboard cladding.

■ **Tip:** In board-and-batten cladding the horizontal battening is sufficient as a support structure. There is no need for ventilation battens as the air cross section between the covering board and the inner board runs vertically and provides adequate ventilation for the outer skin (see Fig. 44).

■ **Tip:** In board-and-batten cladding the boards should be placed with the heartwood side (see Chapter Building material, Timber moisture) facing outwards, so that when the boards deform (bow) as they dry the joint between the floor and covering boards remains closed.

Fig. 44: Vertical cladding – lidded, coverstrip, strip and matchboard cladding

Matchboard cladding

In matchboard cladding, the boards are joined by rebating or tongue-and-groove joints. This means that the boards can be fixed invisibly by concealed nails in the tongue or by using metal clamps. The boards must be left scope for movement by appropriate play in the connection between the boards. For matchboard cladding, additional boards or strips are needed to cover the open corner. In other forms of vertical cladding the corner is closed by a system of double layers of boards or strips. > Fig. 45 ○

Horizontal cladding includes: > Fig. 46

- Lap-joint cladding
- Shiplap cladding

And under certain circumstances:

- Timber shingle cladding
- Strip cladding
- Panel cladding

○ **Note:** Claddings in which the gap between the cladding units is closed are called closed cladding, contrasting with open cladding, which has open joints. For open cladding, windproofing must take the form of a moisture barrier to prevent precipitation water from penetrating the thermal insulation.

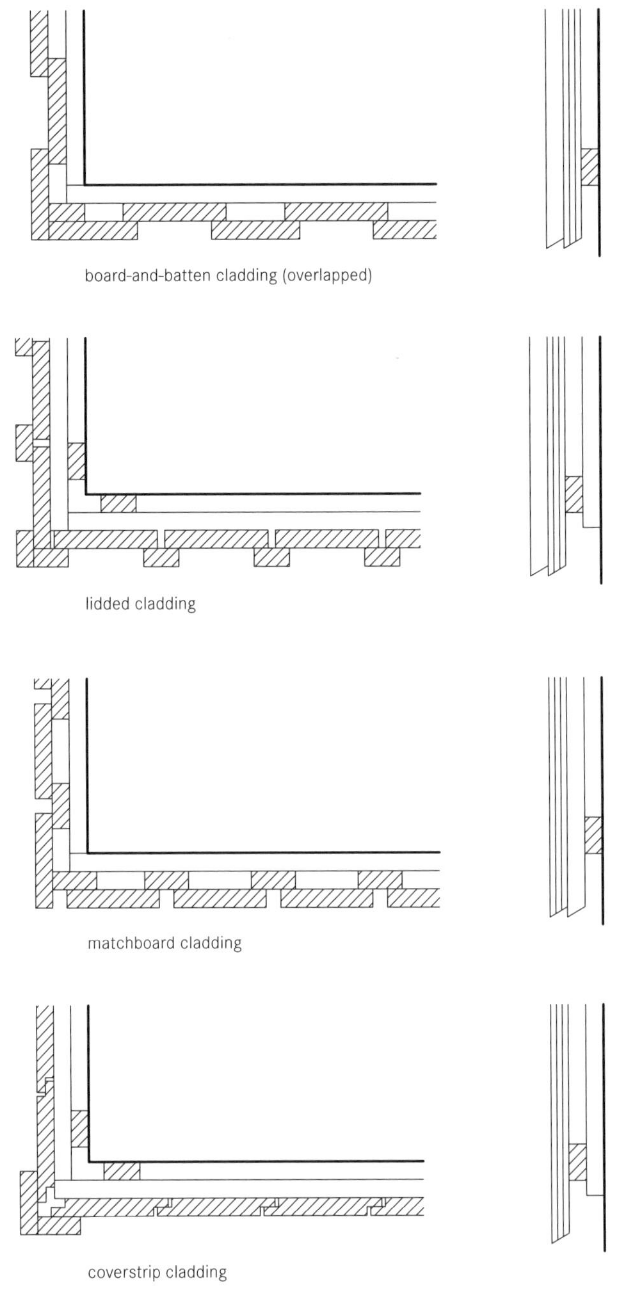

Fig. 45: Vertical cladding

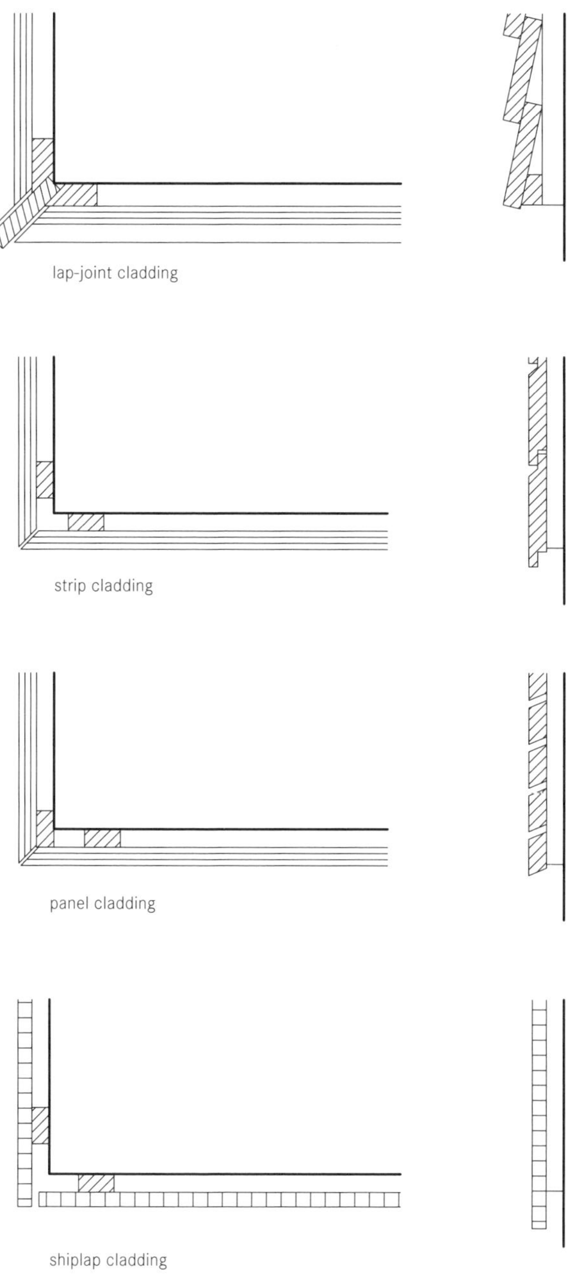

Fig. 46: Horizontal cladding

Fig. 47: Horizontal cladding – lap-joint, shiplap, timber shingle, strip cladding

Lap-joint cladding

The overlap in lap-joint cladding should be 12% of the board width, and at least 10 mm. The cladding boards are not usually rebated, but lap-joint cladding that is rebated in the overlap area does exist.

In lap-joint and board-and-batten cladding the overlapping principle provides scope for distributing the boards evenly over the surface of the wall and the points at which it meets doors and windows.

The diagonal placing of the boards in lap-joint cladding produces a geometrically difficult intersection at a mitred corner. This is often avoided by fitting a vertical board at the corner, to provide a finish for the cladding boards. > Fig. 46

Shiplap cladding

In contrast, a mitred corner is easily executed in shiplap cladding, and so is the concealed fixing. As in matchboard cladding, this can be carried out either with special metal clamps or by nailing or screwing in the tongue. > Figs. 46 and 47 ■

■ **Tip:** In the context of structural timber protection (see Chapter Building material, Timber protection), horizontal cladding, unlike vertical cladding, offers the advantage that a damaged board at base level can easily be replaced. This is particularly important in the case of a shortfall in base height and exposed base areas.

Timber shingle cladding

Timber shingle cladding is executed with small-format timber boards that are nailed or screwed like scales to supporting battens. > Fig. 47, centre right The intricate nature of this format (widths of 50–350 mm and lengths of 120–800 mm) means that it is easier to design curved forms or soft transitions. Timber shingles are available commercially sawn or split. Split shingles last longer, as the cell structure is not damaged by the splitting process. Gaps of 1–5 mm are left between the shingles to allow for swelling. They are often laid in two or three layers. Larch is an excellent timber for making timber shingles. If the roof is pitched steeply enough (30–40°), timber shingles can also be used for roof cladding.

Strip cladding

Strip cladding is a form of open cladding because the gaps are not covered. > Figs. 46 and 47 The ventilation space is particularly important here for draining penetrating precipitation water away. In this case, the windproofing protecting the thermal insulation must also act as a moisture barrier. It makes sense to bevel the strips for structural timber protection. Strip cladding can also run vertically; bevelling the strips is then unnecessary.

Panel cladding

When using panel cladding, care must be taken to choose materials of the correct gluing class for the weather conditions. > Chapter Building material, Timber-based products Timber-based products made of the following materials are suitable for external cladding:

- Veneered plywood
- Three-ply sheets of coniferous timber
- Cement-bound chipboard

The edges of the timber products present a particular problem for panel cladding. One reliable solution is to cover the joints with a cover strip. This protects the sensitive panel edges. Some architects emphasize the structure of the cover strips in the facade by using strips of a different colour from the panels.

The flat, smooth effect made by panel cladding is most effective if the panel joints are executed as dummy joints. In this case the panels must be at least 10 mm apart. The panel edges must be protected from the effects of damp by water-resistant paint.

For horizontal joints, the underside of the panel should be undercut at an angle of inclination of 15°, so that any water running down can drip off. It must also be ensured that no water can stand on the upper edges of the panels. In addition, these edges must be covered, ideally with a metal element that is correspondingly angled outwards at 15°. > Fig. 48

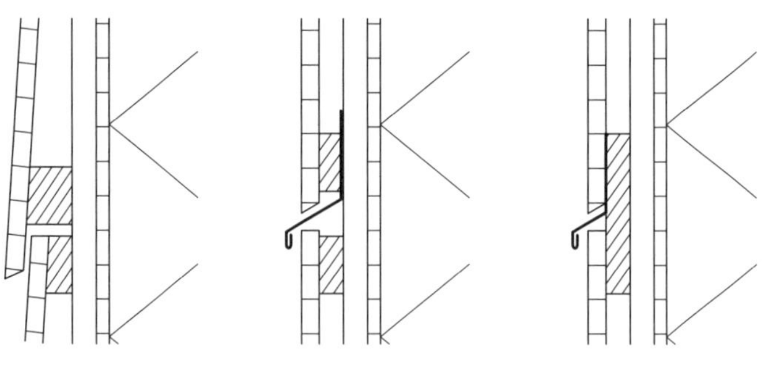

Fig. 48: Horizontal joint

The panels are usually fixed with visible stainless steel screws. A special substructure for hanging the panels is needed for invisible fixing. Systems are available commercially for this.

If the corners consist of a butted joint, as shown in Figure 46, care should be taken that the open edge does not face the prevailing weather. ○

Surface treatment

As external cladding is neither loadbearing nor dimensionally stable it does not need treatment with chemical timber preservatives. > Chapter Building material, Timber protection

But physical timber protection is an option. This is intended to prevent intolerable quantities of precipitation water from being absorbed by the timber and to prevent the surface from UV radiation. Physical timber protection with pigmented transparent coatings or opaque paints prevents the timber surface from greying with time.

Greying

Timber greying is only a colour change: the timber is not actually damaged. Some architects deliberately use timber greying as a design device. For example, the timber surfaces of the Sea Ranch by architects MLTW (Moore, Lyndon, Turnbull & Whitaker) on the west coast of America > photograph, page 73 have acquired a silver-grey patina over the decades from

○ **Note:** As panel cladding is highly sensitive, preventive timber protection measures are advisable to reduce the impact of the weather, through the way the building faces, large roof overhangs or continuous balcony panels.

UV rays and the weathering impact of the ocean, both of which have helped to make these buildings appear at one with nature. When planning detail, care should be taken that protrusions and recesses in the facade do not produce different weathering, and thus possibly undesirable colour effects.

Colour coating

An alternative here is to treat the timber with a coloured coating. Scandinavian timber buildings with strongly coloured paintwork show the impact such treatment can make.

Pigmented transparent coatings and opaque paints are both suitable for colouring timber. As a rule, painting schemes include undercoat, intermediate coat and topcoat. The crucial factor here is that the products used must be compatible with each other. ■

Internal cladding and service installation

Board cladding is one possible option for internal cladding, but timber products such as plywood can also be used. The sound insulation properties of the external wall are improved by one or two layers of plasterboard covering, also called dry-wall finish, because of their comparatively high gross density.

The internal cladding is applied either directly to the loadbearing structure or, preferably, fixed with battening underneath, thus making it simpler to position vertically, as well as enabling ventilation in the case of timber cladding.

Services layer

Installation work on the outside wall generally poses a problem for timber construction. To avoid penetrating the skin, which is closed in terms of building science (vapour- and airtight), all plumbing, heating and electrical services should be kept away from the outside wall and accommodated on inside walls wherever possible. But as it is almost impossible to avoid service runs in the external wall, they are housed in their own course in front of the vapour seal course. Space for pipework

■ **Tip:** Cladding boards should be painted before assembly so that untreated areas do not appear when the timbers shrink. They should be painted with at least the undercoat on both sides to prevent the boards from bowing (see Chapter Building material, Wood).

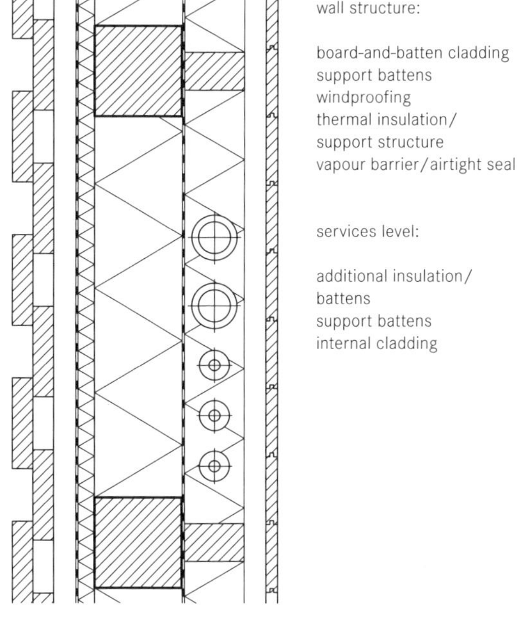

Fig. 49: Services duct

cross sections can be created by increasing the size of the batten structure to 4 or 6 cm. This internal shell can be used as an additional thermal insulation layer. Dedicated services walls and ducts should be planned for bathrooms and wet cells. > Fig. 49

Apertures

The wall's layered structure with windproofing, thermal insulation, vapour barriers and elements to ensure airtightness must be attached to apertures like doors and windows logically and carefully to avoid compromising the structural skin's effectiveness. The transition from the timber cladding deserves particular attention in terms of design as well.

The relatively highly profiled outer skin of lap-joint cladding is shown in detail in Figure 50 left, concluding in a frame running round all four sides, attached rigidly to the window frame. This board is placed diagonally at the lintel and the sill, so that rainwater can run down and drip off.

Ventilation

Ventilation for the timber cladding should also be ensured at the points where windows are attached. It must be possible for air to exit at the sill and enter at the lintel, and the ventilation space must be protected with an insect grille.

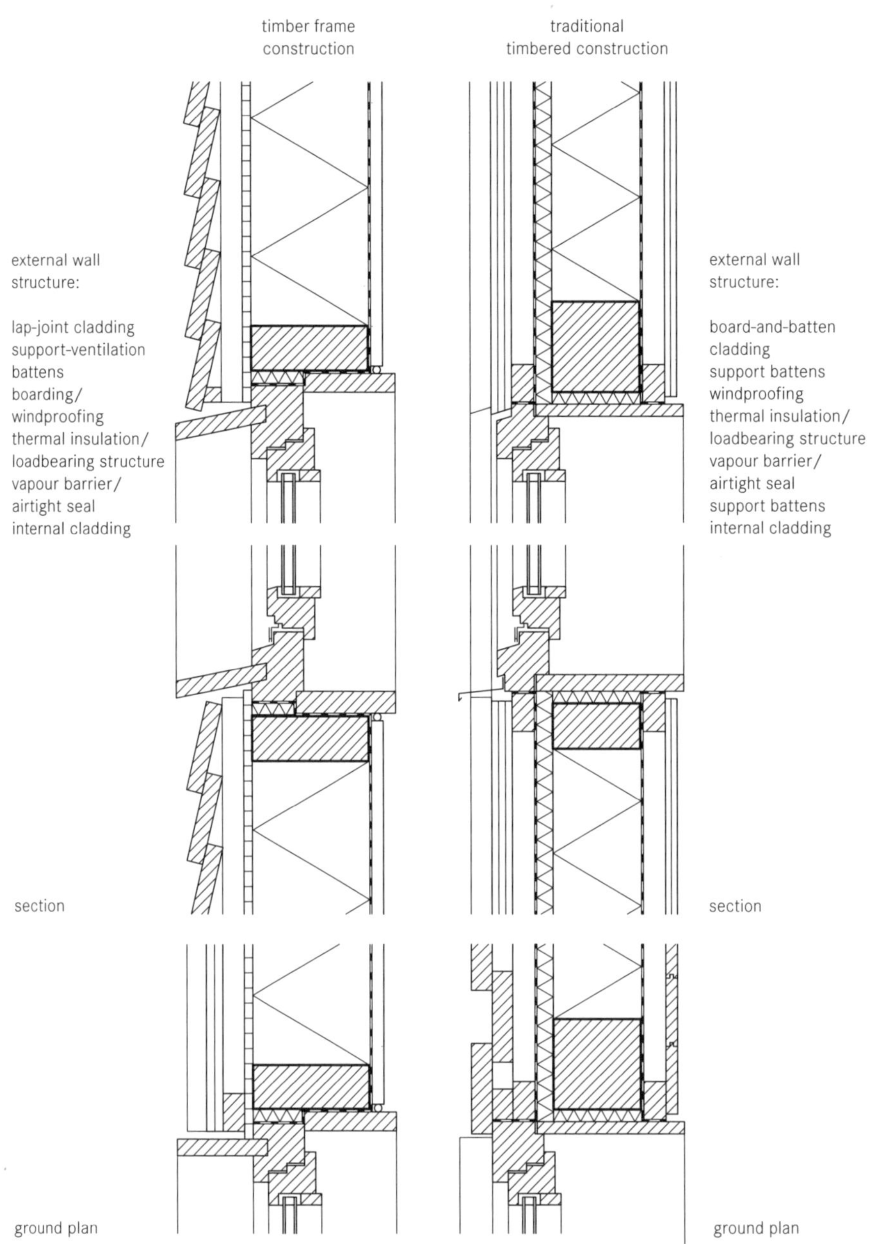

Fig. 50: Facade details window timber frame construction – traditional timbered construction

At the internal intersection, the gap between the window frame and the support structure must also be covered by a board running all the way round.

Vapour barrier

The vapour barrier must be attached directly to the window frame here, in the same way as the wind guard outside, and the gap between the window frame and the support structure filled with thermal insulation material.

The detail of a traditional timbered wall with board-and-batten cladding > Fig. 50, right shows that there is no need for a continuous external frame in this case, so the window has been shifted outwards onto the plane of the cladding. The vertical gap between cladding and window is covered with the external cladding board.

Wind sealing

The wind seal film is attached tight to the window frame using a batten. The frame must be rebated at the lintel so that the vertical cladding can be attached.

Inside, the deep reveal is contained by the window frame. The vapour barrier and the internal cladding are attached to this directly. The window positioned outside is attached to the loadbearing structure by galvanized steel brackets.

INTERNAL WALL

Structure

Loadbearing, non-loadbearing

A basic distinction is made between loadbearing and non-loadbearing internal walls.

Loadbearing internal walls carry their own load and that of the ceilings and roof. Reinforcing walls are also classed as loadbearing. They are part of the building's loadbearing system as a whole, and like the external wall must be constructed as a rigid wall plate, either by planking or braces. > Chapter Construction, Loadbearing system The main function of non-loadbearing walls is to divide rooms.

As a rule, internal walls are constructed on the same grid and follow the same structural system as the external wall. The supporting ribs rise through the full height of a floor and are attached to the threshold and header. In a loadbearing wall, the header supports the ceiling joists. The space between the ceiling joists is finished like the internal wall structure.

Unlike the external wall, the main function of the internal walls is to protect against noise and fire. Thermal insulation is not a factor for walls dividing heated spaces inside the building, and their thickness does not have to take this into account.

Noise protection

The sound insulation value of a wall is determined in the first place by its weight per unit area. The sound insulation performance of an internal wall is raised according to the thickness of the planking with materials of the highest possible gross density, like plaster- or chipboard. Cavity damping, in which the panel cavities are filled with mineral or coconut fibre, makes a considerable contribution to sound insulation. It is sufficient to confine this to half to two thirds of the wall thickness, leaving room for service runs. The internal wall remains open on one side until the services are fully installed. If cellulose is being used for insulation, the insulating flakes cannot be blown in until the chamber is closed. If a particularly high level of sound insulation is needed, a double-leaf wall structure is required. Here, one leaf is articulated, preventing sound transmission from one side of the space to the other. ○

Fixing

Particular care must be taken when fixing the internal wall to the external wall. Both the external and the internal walls must be anchored non-positively, and an adequate basis for the internal cladding must be secured at the inside corner.

In timber frame building the walls are usually attached independently of the structural grid and determined solely by functional room division. Two additional posts are built into the external wall to enable a non-positive connection with the external wall, and also to create a means of fixing the internal wall cladding. > Fig. 22, page 43 and Fig. 51

In traditional timbered building the distribution of the internal walls is matched to the construction grid for the loadbearing posts, so the wall junction lies on the axis of a timber frame post. This post is reinforced on both sides with a wall stud to which the internal cladding is attached. > Fig. 52

○ **Note:** In damp spaces, specially glued timber-product panels or impregnated wallboard, identified by its green colouring in Germany, must be used. Gypsum fibreboard can be used without additional treatment in damp areas. Two layers of wallboard panels are required to support tiles if the ribs are more than 42 cm apart.

In log construction, the connection between the internal and external wall is made, similarly to the outer corner, with an overlap joint. The two walls are anchored so that they are tensionproof with a cog or a dovetail joint. > Chapter Construction, Log construction The dovetail joint creates a characteristic feature for the internal wall because the end-grain is visible on the outside. > Fig. 53

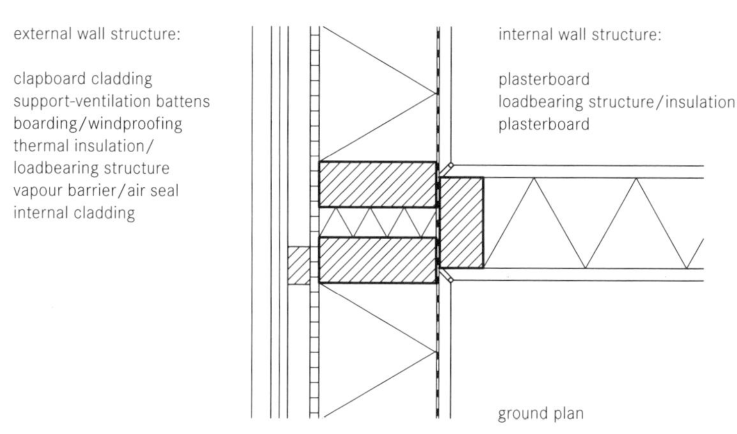

Fig. 51: Internal wall junction in timber frame construction

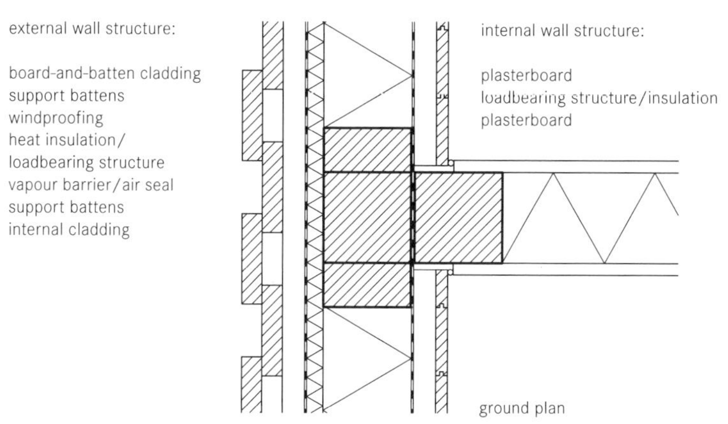

Fig. 52: Internal wall junction in traditional timbered construction

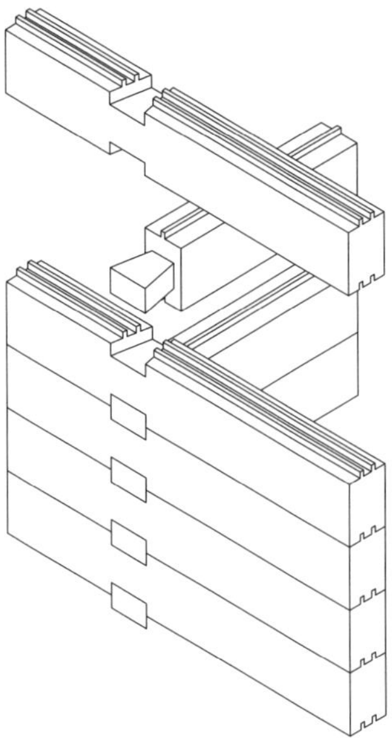

Fig. 53: Internal wall junction in log construction

CEILINGS

Timber ceilings can be constructed using either joists or solid wood. Joisted ceilings tend to predominate in traditional stave construction because of their economical use of wood. Ceiling systems made of prefabricated solid timber elements have recently become more common; they ensure speedier assembly, as in timber panel construction.

Joisted ceilings

Sound insulation

Sound insulation is an important factor in the construction of joisted ceilings. We distinguish between structure-borne or impact sound, and airborne sound. Walking on the floor is one way of creating impact sound. Sources of airborne sound transmission include people's voices in a room, sounds from the radio, television or similar sources.

Structure

A distinction is made between single, double and triple ceiling construction in terms of its sound transmission qualities.

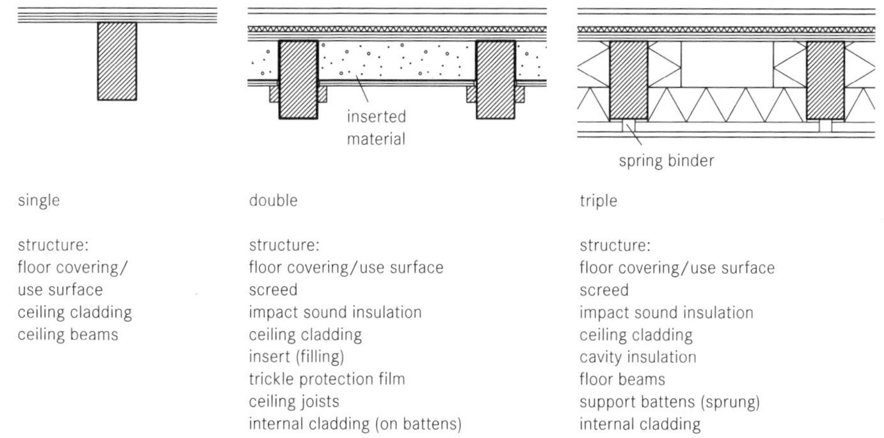

Fig. 54: Single, double and triple structures

Impact sound

In single construction there is direct contact between the floor covering and the support structure, and sound is thus transmitted freely when the floor is walked on.

In double construction the covering and support structure are separated by impact sound insulation. Here, the floor covering needs its own support structure, the screed, which in timber construction is in dry form. For example, dry screeds may be made from double-ply gypsum fibreboard or chipboard. > Fig. 54, Fig. 56, and Chapter Construction, Timber-based products

O

Airborne sound

A triple structure is used to meet extra sound insulation needs, for example to seal bedrooms off from particularly noisy areas. Here, an articulated suspended ceiling is attached to the underside of the joists with spring fasteners (springy strips of sheet metal). This interrupts the direct transmission of sound waves generated by the vibration of the plate.

O **Note:** If the floor covering is separated throughout by the plate and the side walls, we speak of a floating structure. Here, it is important that sound is not transmitted via the walls even at the edges. A peripheral insulation strip should therefore be built in, as well as the horizontally laid impact sound insulation (see Fig. 57, page 85).

The first measure to be taken against sound transmission is to increase weight per unit area. Materials with a relatively high gross density are built into the ceiling, either on top of the ceiling cladding or inserted between the ceiling joists.

Insertion

Specially dried sand is a possible insertion material. > Fig. 54 It is inserted from above into cladding between the ceiling joists. This considerably reduces the visible height of the ceiling joists. A dividing sheet should be used to ensure that the sand does not trickle down through the joints when the ceiling vibrates.

Another way of increasing the weight of the ceiling on the ceiling cladding is to lay concrete paving stones, for example, and glue them firmly to the cladding. They are followed by the remaining floor structure, impact sound insulation, screed and the covering.

Joists

Spacing

When planning a ceiling with timber joists, care should be taken that the beams run parallel with the shorter sides of the room wherever possible. The maximum spacing for solid timber joints is about 5 m. Beams running over two or more fields are more economical than single-field joists.

Dimensioning

The loadbearing capacity of a timber joist is affected more by its height than its width. For this reason, timber joists are installed upright, so as to use the timber cross sections relatively economically. A side ratio of 1:2 or more is usual. The maximum height of squared timber is

○ 240–280 mm.

TJI joists

TJI joists are a particularly efficient and reasonably priced system. They are used above all in American timber construction. The name derives from the manufacturer Truss Joint MacMillan Idaho. The double T structure is made up of solid or veneer plywood chords with a glued-in web of OSB panels. > Chapter Construction, Timber-based products They offer very high loadbearing capacity combined with great lightness. As the members are very high, it is relatively easy to run services across the joists, and space is engineered for this purpose at the factory. TJI-joisted ceilings are usually clad on the underside. > Fig. 55

Space between joists

Joists are usually spaced at 60–70 cm intervals. But in timber construction it makes sense to match the joint spacing to the construction grid, so that where possible the ceiling load can be conducted directly into the loadbearing posts.

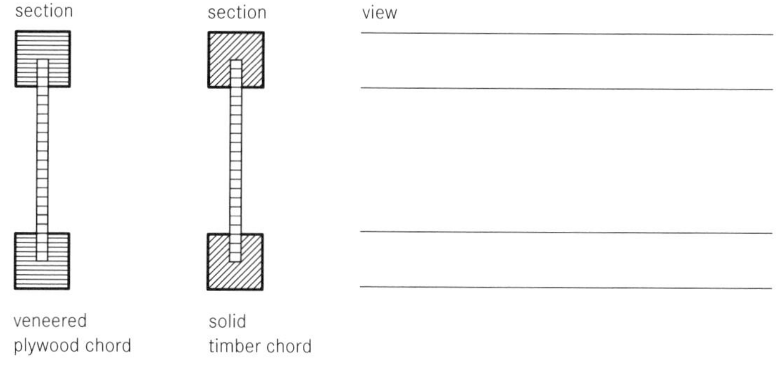

Fig. 55: TJI joist

In most floor-by-floor timber construction systems the walls support the joists. The necessary bearing depth can be calculated as joint height × 0.7.

Trimmers

It is possible to use trimmers with loadbearing joists if they are penetrated by service shafts, chimneys or stairs, as is also the case of rafters in a timber roof truss. > *Basics Roof Construction* Trimmer joists are built in flush with the other joists, and attached to them by mortise and tenon. The joint is usually secured against being pulled out by a metal clamp. For fire prevention, there must be a clearance of 5 cm between the chimney and the timber joists.

Seating

As a detail typical of timber construction, > Fig. 57 the circular peripheral joist forms a kind of frame for the ceiling joists, securing the slender joists against buckling sideways while functioning as a compression and tension member similar to a peripheral tie beam in the system as a whole.

○ **Note:** This formula gives a rough approximation for dimensioning timber-joisted ceilings:

Joist height h = span/20

Greater heights can be achieved only with laminated timber or timber products.

Fig. 56: Ceiling systems – joisted ceiling, joist skeleton construction, TJI joist

To achieve a plate effect in the statical sense, the joists must be planked with panels that are suitable for stiffening, e.g. plywood. Care should be taken to offset the panel joints so that they can be bonded rather like masonry.

Vapour barrier

The continuous vapour barrier running through the external wall poses a particular problem. To prevent interruption of the barrier at the seating, the vapour barrier sheet should be taken round the edge of the ceiling and joined from one floor to the next. Care should also be taken that the layer of insulation is not interrupted or weakened at the seating, to prevent condensation water from accumulating either in the wall or at the seating. > Chapter Components, Building science

Joist hangers/ joist supports

The detail in Figure 58 shows the joists in a traditional timbered construction suspended between the walls. Steel joist hangers or joist supports are needed for this butted junction. These are available commercially in various sizes to suit the building statics. ○

○ **Note:** The use of visible joist hangers depends on whether the timber joist ceiling is clad on the underside. Otherwise, joist supports are used for visible joists. These fit into slots in the joist head and fasten the joist to the external wall using dowel pins placed transversely to the joint head (see Figs. 28 and 56, centre, page 84).

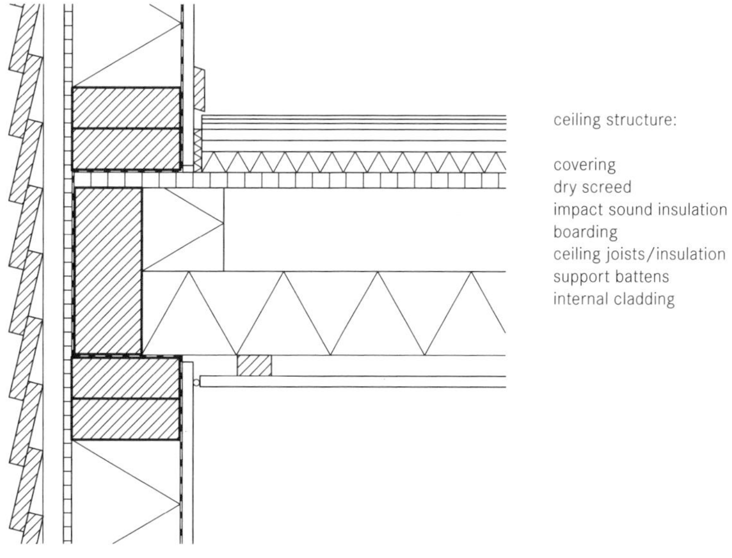

ceiling structure:

covering
dry screed
impact sound insulation
boarding
ceiling joists/insulation
support battens
internal cladding

Fig. 57: Ceiling seating in timber frame construction

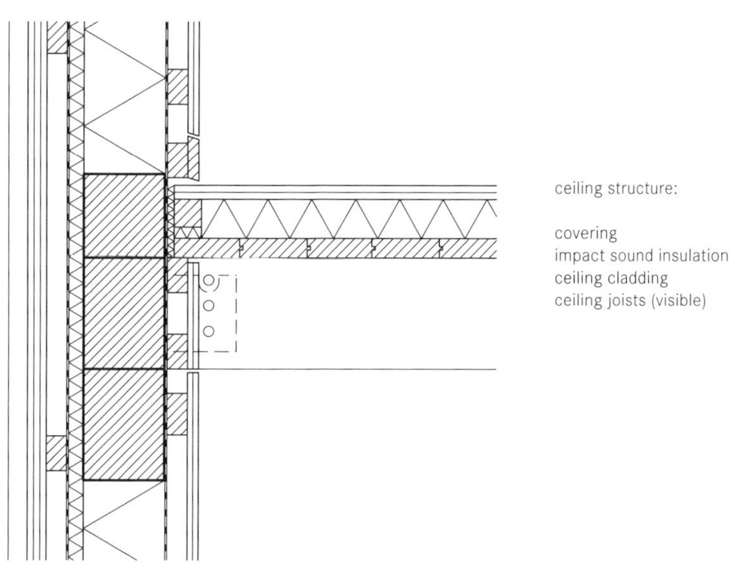

ceiling structure:

covering
impact sound insulation
ceiling cladding
ceiling joists (visible)

Fig. 58: Ceiling seating in traditional timbered construction

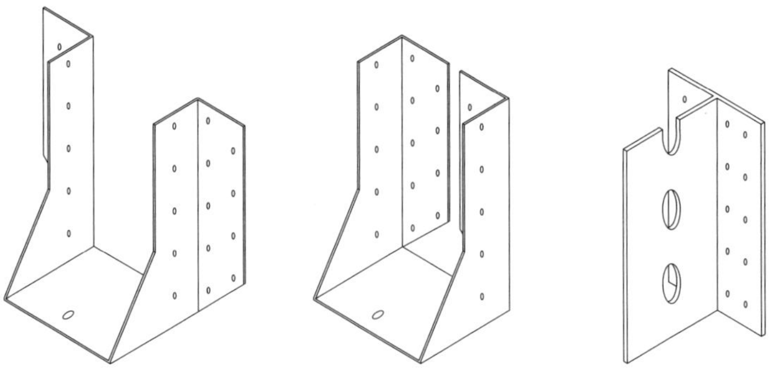

Fig. 59: Joist hangers, joist support

The continuous rail at joist level makes a butted connection possible. In this case, the vapour barrier can run vertically on the same plane, but must be attached to the joist hangers or joist supports in such a way that the structure is vapourtight. In the detail shown a joist support is used because the timber ceiling joists are visible.

Internal seating

If the joists are not suspended as illustrated, but intended to lie on top of the walls, it is possible to create an internal seating in front of the external wall in the form of another internal supporting plane, which can also be used as an additional insulating layer, a services layer, > Fig. 49, page 75 or a substructure for the internal cladding.

Solid ceilings

As timber construction systems developed from log to timber skeleton structures, the quantity of timber used has constantly been reduced. This trend has recently been reversed. > Chapter Construction, Timber panel construction More timber is being used as the technology changes. This applies particularly to intermediate floors, for which a series of new systems have brought the advantages of solid floors.

These advantages include:

- Shorter assembly times
- Simple, usually industrial manufacture
- Thinner cross sections
- Increased thermal and sound insulation between floors

At the same time, the smooth lower edge of the ceiling makes the junction with the walls easier.

The additional structures on top do not differ in principle from those on joisted ceilings, although measures for improving thermal and sound insulation - i.e. inserts between the joists or surface structures to raise the unit area weight - are generally not needed.

Box beams

Solid wood constructions also include box beams, industrially prefabricated from boards and only assembled as a floor on site. They are supplied with a double mortise and tenon to this end. They are particularly suitable when large spans have to be bridged.

Industrial manufacture guarantees a precise fit and quality standard. The box beam units are a standard 195 m wide and are supplied in standard lengths up to 12 m. They are obtainable in heights from 120–280 mm according to span, graduated in 20 mm units.

The standard values in Table 9 apply to a load of 3 kN/m^2.

Tab.9: Standard values for dimensioning box beams

Span	Unit height
3.8 m	120 mm
4.5 m	140 mm
5.2 m	200 mm

Edge-glued construction

The edge-glued construction system uses the side boards from the trunk and cleared small dimension timber unsuitable for beams and squared timber. The boards are laid longitudinally and are joined upright without gluing by side nailing following a fixed nailing scheme to form ceiling or wall elements. Longitudinal joints in the boards have to be staggered. The elements, which are supplied with special rebates, are fastened to the complete section. > Fig. 60

Edge-glued elements must be protected from moisture, particularly during the building period, as water penetrating the boards would create a degree of swelling that is intolerable for any fitting situation.

They are supplied in standard dimensions according to manufacturer: in thicknesses of 100–220 mm, widths of up to 2500 mm and lengths of up to 17 m.

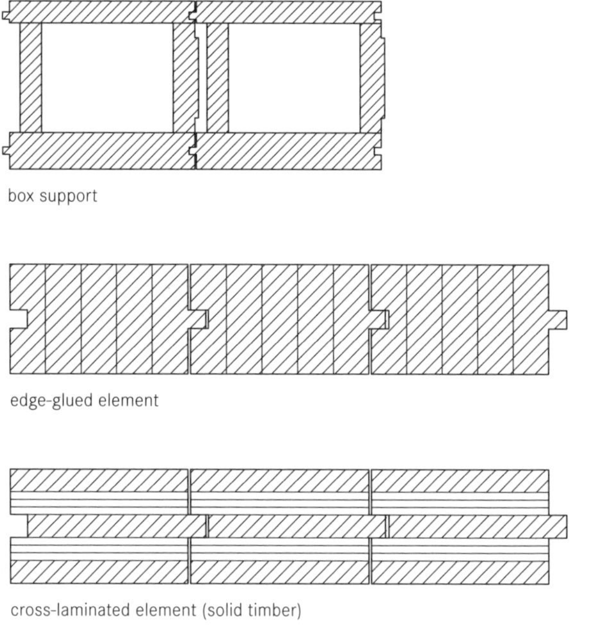

Fig. 60: Box support, edge-glued element, cross-laminated element

The standard values in Table 10 apply to loads of 3 kN/m^2.

Cross-laminated timber

Cross-laminated timber consists of layers of wedge-dovetailed softwood boards 17 or 27 mm thick glued to each other crosswise. The crossing effect makes the elements very stable in terms of form and they are thus suitable for wall construction. The covering layers can also be made of other timber products to improve the surface.

Depending on the covering layer and the number of layers, the panel thicknesses lie between 51 and 297 mm. The maximum width is 4.8 m. The units are made to a maximum length of 20 m to suit the particular purpose. Walls can therefore be built up to four storeys high using this material.

The values given in Table 11 apply to loads of up to 3 kN/m^2.

All the three solid ceiling systems described are also used as solid material for walls, following a similar principle known as solid panel

Tab.10: Standard values for dimensioning edge-glued elements

Span	Unit height
3.6 m	100 mm
4.3 m	120 mm
5.0 m	140 mm

Tab.11: Standard values for dimensioning cross-laminated timber

Span	Unit height
3.8 m	115 mm
4.6 m	142 mm
6.4 m	189 mm

construction. The number of new products on the market in addition the systems described is increasing constantly. > Chapter Solid panel construction

ROOFS

Most masonry buildings include some timber construction. Pitched roofs usually have timber roof trusses, above all in detached house construction. But under close consideration, a timber roof truss on a masonry building represents a hybrid building method combining two different systems, lightweight construction and solid construction, a dry building method and masonry construction using wet mortar. ○

Pitched roofs

In timber structures, the pitched roof and the wall are constructed following a common principle.

○ **Note:** Here the reader is again referred to the volume *Basics Roof Construction* by Ann-Christin Siegemund, in which the terms used below are explained.

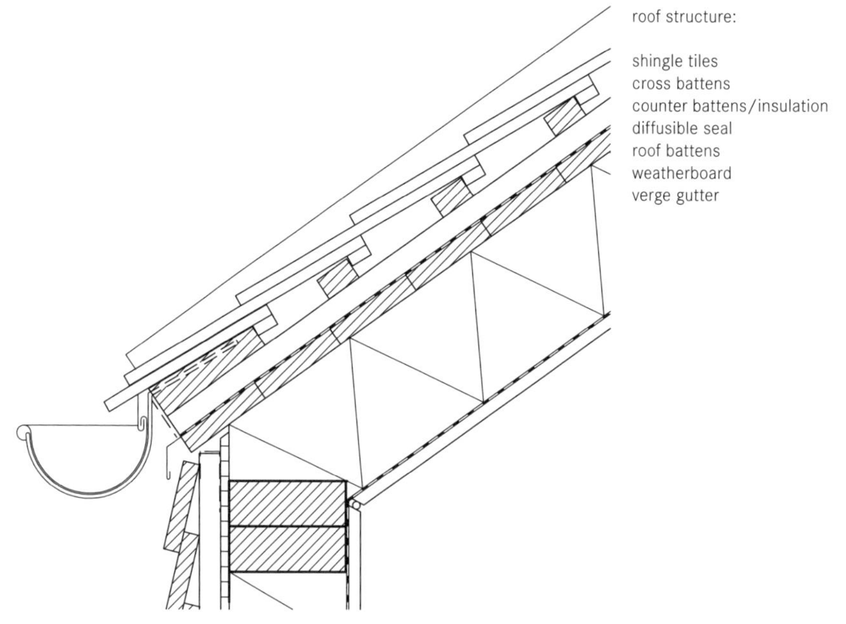

Fig. 61: Eaves without roof overhang

Layers

The functions and sequence of the layers, starting from the outside, weatherproof shell with substructure, sealing or windproofing, insulating layer, vapour barrier and internal cladding, are identical. But the aim is to join these layers at the point of transition from roof to wall to create a continuous envelope that fulfils all the scientific building functions without interruptions or weak points.

Anchorage

In addition, the roof loads from the roof structure's own weight plus snow loads in winter have to be transferred to the external wall. At the same time, the roof is anchored to the outside walls, to be able to absorb wind suction force, to which the roof is particularly susceptible. But as well as these numerous technical demands, design requirements must not be forgotten. The eaves and verge of a building make a particular impact on its architecture. A major issue is whether the roof should be constructed with or without an overhang.

Building science

The detailed section in Figure 61 shows a relatively simple solution to the transition from roof to wall, as all the layers can be merged without

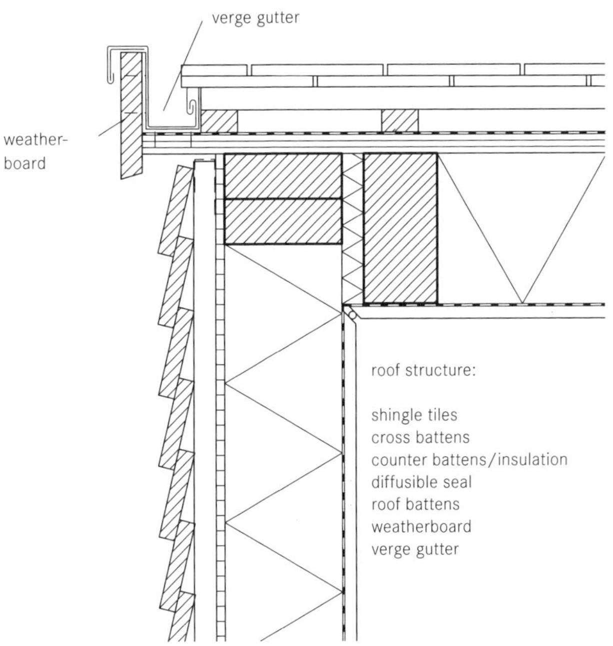

Fig. 62: Verge without roof overhang

difficulty. The internal wallboard cladding on both sections is trimmed off at the edges at the transition point, but the mastic seal is scarcely perceptible in the room if the colour of the wall is matched to the joint.

Gluing the sheeting to the inside corner of the eaves and verge closes the vapour- and airtight envelope of the completed roof space.

The insulation layers between the loadbearing wall posts and the roof rafters are attached to each other directly. The header of the longitudinal wall and the gable wall form the upper conclusion.

Seating

No special purlin is required at the eaves as it is in masonry construction because the rafters can rest directly on the timber frame wall. Care should be taken at the verge to fill the gap between the gable wall and the peripheral rafter tightly with insulating material, to avoid creating a serious thermal bridge. ○

○ **Note:** The gable wall, unlike all the other walls in the building, concludes not with a horizontal header, but with a header running diagonally at the angle of the roof pitch. The verge is cut orthogonally in the plan view to obviate distorted cross sections (see Fig. 62).

Outer skin

For the roof, the full rafter insulation is clad with boarding and a roofing sheet that is open to diffusion ($S_d > 2$ m), and on the wall the stiffening plywood panel forms a conclusion and protects the thermal insulation.

The outer skin of roof and wall is ventilated from the rear. Each air space is entirely independent of the others, a ventilation system in its own right, with separate air in- and outlets.

Roof edge

Not having the roof project emphasizes the volume of the building and makes it a more powerful physical presence. Wall and roof affect the overall impression the building makes almost equally. This impression may be enhanced by the related scale principle of the lap-joint cladding on the wall and the flat-tail shingle tiles on the roof.

The gable edge of the roof is particularly exposed to the wind, and is protected by a weatherboard. As screwing into the end-grain timber of the roof cladding is not permissible, the weatherboard is fastened to the roof cladding with a galvanized flat steel tie. Any precipitation appearing between the roof covering and the weatherboard is collected in a sheet metal verge gutter and directed to the eaves and into the roof guttering.

Roof projection

The building makes a very different spatial impression with a roof projection. The projecting roof is more clearly detached from the body of the building and seems to have more of a life of its own. The different material language used for the roof covering and the wall cladding emphasizes the autonomy of both buildings.

The roof projection running round all four sides is important in protecting the wall cladding from precipitation and contributes considerably to structural timber protection for the building. A corresponding disadvantage is that the rafters penetrate the outer skin. But the bevelling means that the rafter end is relatively well protected under the roof skin and the more delicate end-grain wood is not directly exposed to the weather.

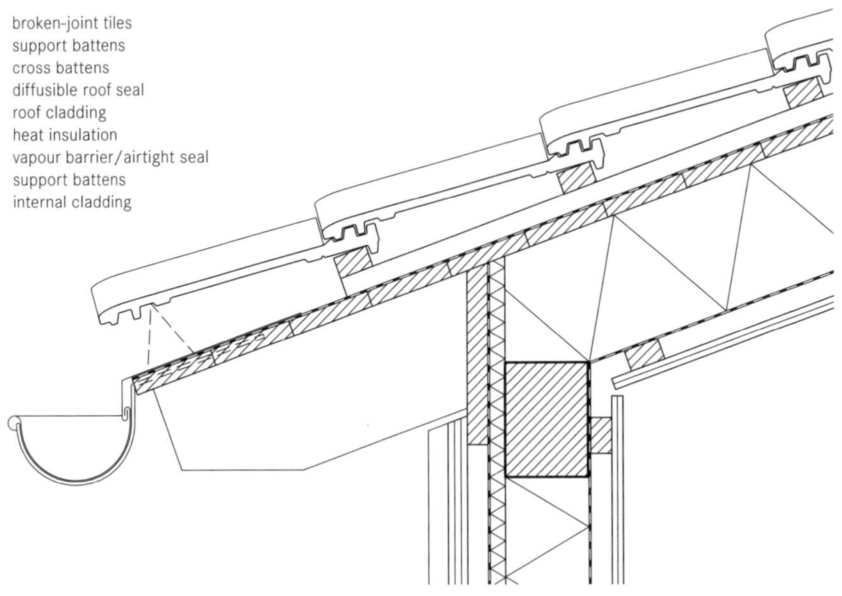

Fig. 63: Eaves with projecting roof

Wall junction

In order to avoid laboriously matching the vertical board-and-batten cladding to the rafters, the cladding ends at their lower edge. A board is inserted between the rafters to cope with this; > Figs. 63 and 64 it also fixes the upper edge of the cladding. Ventilation behind the external cladding finds an outlet via the air space between the inner board and the covering board.

Verge

At the verge, however, the wall cladding follows the edge of the roof, and extends to just under the roof cladding, where a gap of 2–3 cm is needed to ensure that air from the ventilation system can escape.

The roof projection on the gable side can be achieved only with protruding purlins. These support the outer rafter, called the verge rafter, which cannot be supported inside the building, but by the timber frame of the longitudinal wall. It runs out beyond the gable wall as an eaves purlin and thus continues to support the verge rafter. The framing timber should be dimensioned according to the width of the protrusion. It is better to replace the square cross section with an upright beam format.

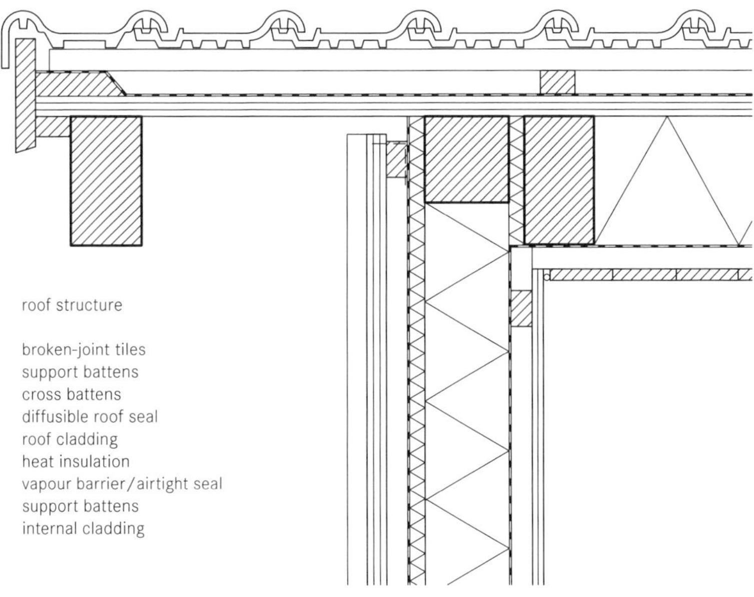

Fig. 64: Verge with projecting roof

The verge detail shown in Figure 64 differs from flat shingle tiling as no verge gutter is needed. A specially shaped verge tile removes the water. It and the weatherboard conclude and protect the roof cladding. The weatherboard is screwed at the side to strips reinforcing the upper and lower sides of the edge of the cladding.

Flat roofs

Flat roofs are a key feature of modern architecture. They are generally used in the context of concrete structures. The flat roof is now also accepted as part of modern timber construction.

Parapet

In the detail shown in Figure 65 the external skin extends to the end of the roof as bevelled cladding, also sometimes called the parapet in the case of flat roofs. There is no need of a weatherboard to protect the roof skin, as used for the pitched roof gable, as this role is performed by the roof parapet, which protrudes at least 10 cm beyond the roof skin. This parapet and the open-top facade cladding are protected by sheet metal cladding angled inwards. Air from the facade's ventilation must be able to escape at this point.

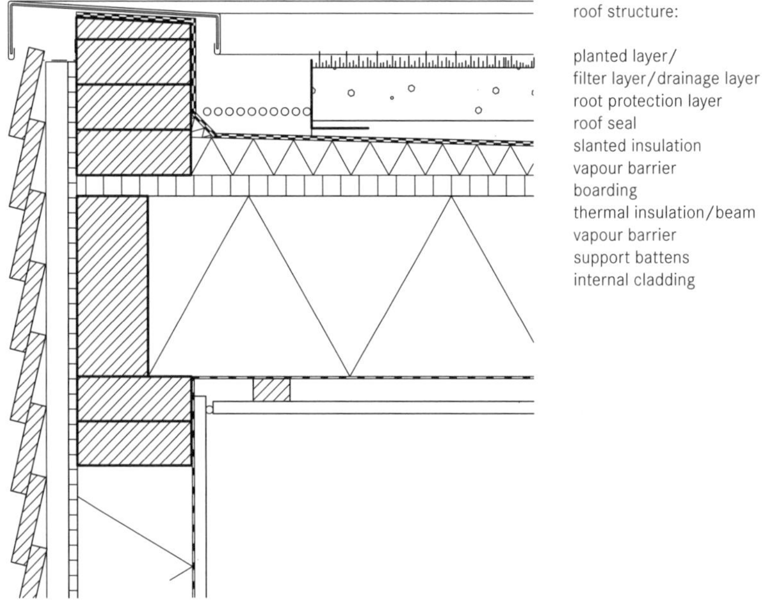

Fig. 65: Flat roof edge joisted ceiling – timber frame construction

Seating

The roof ceiling is constructed and seated in the same way as the intermediate floors. > Fig. 57, page 85 The roof parapet, made up of two horizontal timber cross sections is reminiscent of the threshold running round the intermediate floors.

As in the external wall, the insulation is placed between the supporting joists of the roof. But as the rest of the structure is conceived as an unventilated flat roof, the vapour barrier on the inside of the roof insulation has a very particular part to play. An additional, inclined layer of insulation material is fixed to the roof cladding, to ensure a continuous slope on the firmly rooted roof seal down to the roof gullies. This is best achieved with piled granular material. This insulation later also bridges possible weak points in the roof insulation below.

The low degree of storage afforded by a lightweight flat roof can be compensated for with a green roof. A strip of gravel at least 50 cm wide must separate the planting from the edge of the flat roof and the timber building components, for fire protection reasons.

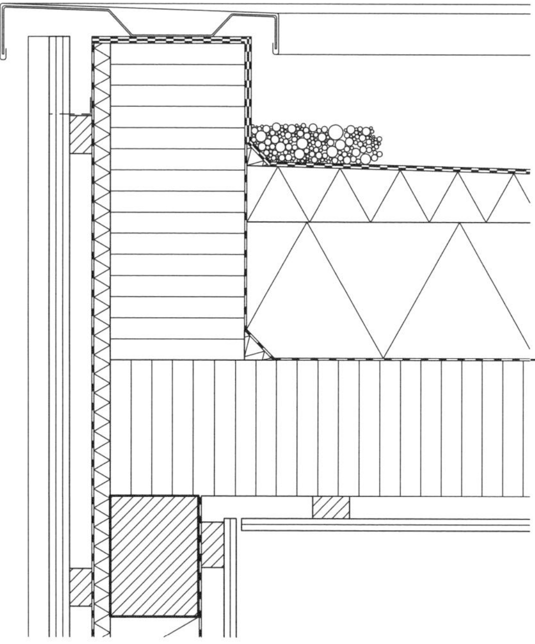

Fig. 66: Flat roof edge: Edge-glued ceiling – traditional timbered structure

The flat roof edges shown in Figures 65 and 66 each show only one of the many possible detailed solutions for the external design for the roof edge, as well as for the structure of the roof itself.

It should also be remembered that although an unventilated construction is a very common solution, flat roofs can also be constructed with ventilation, like pitched roofs.

A roof ceiling that uses edge-glued construction > Chapter Components, Ceilings is very close to a flat roof construction in solid reinforced concrete, in structure as well as in detail.

Solid wood construction helps to improve thermal insulation and the storage efficiency of the roof. The edge-glued elements are supported by the frame of the timbered wall, and the slope up to the roof parapet is also constructed using edge-glued elements.

Structure

A ventilated roof structure will be used above the solid wood ceiling, similarly to a reinforced concrete flat roof. Here, the vapour barrier is laid on the roof ceiling below the thermal insulation. The insulation layers of wall and roof are connected only indirectly via the solid timber components. The external thermal insulation layer in front of the loadbearing structure prevents thermal bridges from being formed.

In conclusion

At the end of our *Basics Timber Construction* volume it is fitting to emphasize timber's special qualities as a building material once again. In the Tectonics chapter of his book *Style,* Gottfried Semper called it the "primeval material of all stave constructions".

Timber construction means building elementally according to constructive logic and clear, easily understood laws. Differently from solid structures, the flow of forces in stave structures can be read and studied directly.

Understanding timber construction also opens the way to understanding many other construction systems used by architects. There is an immediate sense of parallels with steel construction, with joints of bars and surfaces. Something similar applies to metal and glass facades, which have taken over timber construction's post and rail approach. And even concrete, as a cast material, draws on the tectonic principles of timber construction for its loadbearing systems made up of columns, beams and ribs. The loadbearing effect of a reinforced concrete ceiling can be more readily understood if the reinforcing role of the loadbearing steel bars is translated mentally into timber beams.

Many architecture courses start with timber construction, for this reason. For example, it helps with understanding fundamental construction principles and is a multifaceted and unique field in which to work.

Appendix

STANDARDS

Timber construction in general

DIN EN 338	Timber structures - strength classes
DIN EN 384	Structural timber - determination of characteristic values of mechanical properties and density
DIN EN 1995	Design of timber structures
DIN V ENV 1995-1-1 Eurocode 5:	design of timber structures; Part 1-1: general rules and rules for building
AS 1684.1-3 1999	Residential timber - framed construction - Design criteria
AS 1720.1 1997	Timber structures - Design methods

Timber as a building material

DIN EN 338	Loadbearing construction timber - strength classes
DIN EN 384	Loadbearing construction timber - definition of characteristic strength, rigidity and bulk density values
DIN EN 1912	Loadbearing construction timber - strength classes - classification of visual sorting classes and timber types

Timber protection

DIN EN 335	Durability of wood and derived materials; definition of hazard classes of biological attack
DIN EN 350	Durability of wood and wood-based products
DIN EN 351	Durability of wood and wood-based products - preservative-treated solid wood

Waterproofing

DIN 18531	Waterproofing for utilized and non-utilized roofs
DIN 18533	Waterproofing of elements in contact with soil
DIN 18534	Waterproofing for indoor applications

US Standards

Uniform building code, UBC

UBC V, Chapter 25 Wood

Handbook to the Uniform Building Code Part V Capter 25 Wood - An illustrative commentary

Wood - Frame House Construction, United States Department of Agriculture, Forest Service

Wood Handbook, United States Department of Agriculture, Forest Service

LITERATURE

American Institute of Timber Construction (AITC): *Timber Construction Manual,* John Wiley & Sons, Hoboken/NJ 2012

Werner Blaser: *Holz-Haus. Maisons de bois. Wood Houses,* Wepf, Basel 1980

Francis D. K. Ching: *Building Construction Illustrated,* 5th edition, John Wiley & Sons, Hoboken/NJ 2014

Andrea Deplazes (ed.): *Constructing Architecture,* Birkhäuser, Basel 2013

Keith F. Faherty, Thomas G. Williamson: *Wood Engineering and Construction Handbook*, McGraw-Hill Professional, New York 1998

Manfred Hegger, Volker Auch-Schwelk, Matthias Fuchs, Thorsten Rosenkranz: *Construction Materials Manual,* Birkhäuser, Basel 2006

Thomas Herzog, Michael Volz, Julius Natterer, Wolfgang Winter, Roland Schweizer: *Timber Construction Manual*, Birkhäuser, Basel 2003

Theodor Hugues, Ludwig Steiger, Johann Weber: *Timber Construction,* Birkhäuser, Basel 2004

Wolfgang Ruske: *Timber Construction for Trade, Industry, Administration*, Birkhäuser, Basel 2004

William P. Spence: *Residential Framing,* Sterling Publishing Co., New York 1993

Anton Steurer: *Developments in Timber Engineering,* Birkhäuser, Basel 2006

PICTURE CREDITS

Figure page 12: Johann Weber
Figure page 28: Ludwig Steiger
Figure 14: Ludwig Steiger
Figure 23: Jörg Weber
Figures 30–37: Jörg Rehm
Figure page 55: Ludwig Steiger
Figure 44: Anja Riedl
Figure 47: Anja Riedl/Jörg Rehm
Figure 56: Ludwig Steiger/Jörg Weber
Figure page 73: Ludwig Steiger
Figure page 93: Architekturbüro Fischer + Steiger
Drawings: Florian Müller/Jörg Rehm

THE AUTHOR

Ludwig Steiger, Dipl.-Ing. Univ., architect, is a lecturer in building construction and interior fitting-out at TU München and co-owner of the Fischer + Steiger architectural practice in Munich.

Jörg Rehm, Dr.-Ing., TU Munich, Contribution to Chap. *Timber panel construction*

ALSO AVAILABLE FROM BIRKHÄUSER:

Design
Basics Barrierfree Planning
Isabella Skiba, Rahel Züger
ISBN 978-3-0356-2192-1

Basics Design and Living
Jan Krebs
ISBN 978-3-0356-1663-7

Basics Office Design
Bert Bielefeld
ISBN 978-3-0356-1394-0

Basics Design Ideas
Bert Bielefeld, Sebastian El khouli
ISBN 978-3-0356-1745-0

Basics Design Methods
Kari Jormakka
ISBN 978-3-03821-520-2

Basics Materials
M. Hegger, H. Drexler, M. Zeumer
ISBN 978-3-0356-2184-6

Basics Spatial Design
Ulrich Exner, Dietrich Pressel
ISBN 978-3-0356-2019-1

Available as a compendium:
Basics Architectural Design
Bert Bielefeld (ed.)
ISBN 978-3-03821-560-8

Fundamentals of Presentation
Basics Architectural Photography
Michael Heinrich
ISBN 978-3-7643-8666-5

Basics CAD
Jan Krebs
ISBN 978-3-7643-8109-7

Basics Freehand Drawing
Florian Afflerbach
ISBN 978-3-03821-545-5

Basics Detail Drawing
Bert Bielefeld (ed.)
ISBN 978-3-0356-1392-6

Basics Freehand Drawing
Florian Afflerbach
ISBN 978-3-03821-545-5

Basics Modelbuilding
Alexander Schilling
ISBN 978-3-0356-2186-0

Basics Technical Drawing
Bert Bielefeld, Isabella Skiba
ISBN 978-3-0346-1326-2

Available as a compendium:
Basics Architectural Presentation
Bert Bielefeld (ed.)
ISBN 978-3-03821-527-1

Construction
Basics Concrete Construction
Katrin Hanses
ISBN 978-3-0356-0362-0

Basics Facade Apertures
Roland Krippner, Florian Musso
ISBN 978-3-7643-8466-1

Basics Glass Construction
Andreas Achilles, Diane Navratil
ISBN 978-3-7643-8851-5

Basics Loadbearing Systems
Alfred Meistermann
ISBN 978-3-0356-2188-4

Basics Masonry Construction
Nils Kummer
ISBN 978-3-7643-7645-1

Basics Roof Construction
Ann-Christin Siegemund
ISBN 978-3-0356-1942-3

Basics Steel Construction
Katrin Hanses
ISBN 978-3-0356-0370-5

Available as a compendium:
Basics Building
Construction
Bert Bielefeld (ed.)
ISBN 978-3-0356-0372-9

Building Services/
Building Physics
Basics Fire Safety
Diana Helmerking
ISBN 978-3-0356-1859-4

Basics Lighting Design
Roman Skowranek
ISBN 978-3-0356-0929-5

Basics Electro-Planning
Peter Wotschke
ISBN 978-3-0356-0932-5

Basics Room Conditioning
Oliver Klein, Jörg Schlenger
ISBN 978-3-7643-8664-1

Basics Water Cycles
Doris Haas-Arndt
ISBN 978-3-7643-8854-6

Available as a compendium:
Basics Building Technology
Bert Bielefeld (ed.)
ISBN 978-3-0356-0928-8

Professional Practice
Basics Project Control
Pecco Becker
ISBN 978-3-0356-1666-8

Basics Budgeting
Bert Bielefeld, Roland Schneider
ISBN 978-3-03821-532-5

Basics Construction Scheduling
Bert Bielefeld
ISBN 978-3-7643-8873-7

Basics Site Management
Lars-Phillip Rusch
ISBN 978-3-0356-1607-1

Basics Tendering
Tim Brandt,
Sebastian Th. Franssen
ISBN 978-3-0356-2187-7

Basics Construction Scheduling
Bert Bielefeld
ISBN 978-3-7643-8873-7

Available as a compendium:
Basics Project Management
Architecture
Bert Bielefeld (ed.)
ISBN 978-3-03821-462-5

Urbanism
Basics Urban Analysis
Gerrit Schwalbach
ISBN 978-3-7643-8938-3

Basics Urban Building Blocks
Thorsten Bürklin, Michael Peterek
ISBN 978-3-7643-8460-9

Available at your bookshop or at
www.birkhauser.com

Series editor: Bert Bielefeld
Concept: Bert Bielefeld, Annette Gref
Translation from German into English:
Michael Robinson, Hartwin Busch
English copy editing: Monica Buckland,
Patricia Kot
Project management: Annette Gref
Layout, cover design, and typography:
Andreas Hidber
Typesetting: Sven Schrape
Production: Amelie Solbrig

Paper: Magno Natural, 120 g/m²
Print: Beltz Grafische Betriebe GmbH

Library of Congress Control Number:
2020938914

Bibliographie information published by the
German National Library

The German National Library lists this publication in the Deutsche Nationalbibliografie; detailed bibliographic data are available on the Internet at http://dnb.dnb.de.

ISBN 978-3-0356-2126-6
e-ISBN (PDF) 978-3-0356-2127-3
e-ISBN (EPUB) 978-3-0356-2131-0
German Print-ISBN 978-3-0356-2124-2
French Print-ISBN 978-3-0356-2125-9

P.O. Box 44, 4009 Basel, Switzerland
Part of Walter de Gruyter GmbH, Berlin/Boston

9 8 7 6 5 4 3 2

www.birkhauser.com